The Story of

JONAS MAPES

GENERAL JONAS MAPES (1768–1827)
Portrait by Samuel L. Waldo

The Story of

JONAS MAPES

An Early-Nineteenth-Century
New Yorker

H A R R Y   W.   H A V E M E Y E R

PRIVATELY PRINTED, NEW YORK

Published in the United States

ISBN-10: 1-931648-03-4

Printed and bound in the United States
First Edition

Set in Adobe Caslon Pro
Design by Nick Caruso

To the many descendants of General Mapes

PREFACE
ix

INTRODUCTION
xi

PART I
On Long Island

PART II
In New York City

EPILOGUE
147

SOURCE NOTES
157

INDEX
160

PREFACE

As was his life, the story of Jonas Mapes can be divided into two parts. The first part covers his ancestry going back to five families that came to the New World and eventually to Long Island in the 1630s, as well as his youth in Mattituck on Long Island's North Fork. The second begins with his move to New York City when he was twenty years old, his career as a merchant tailor and an officer of the New York State militia, his rise to major general with the defense of New York City against an expected second invasion by the British Army in 1814, and finally, his senior years in a city rapidly expanding due to the completion of the Erie Canal in 1825. Unlike many of the early figures in New York, Mapes was not a member of the landed gentry and never accumulated much wealth to pass along to his family. Nevertheless, he became an elected alderman of the city and a prominent officer in the militia. In both capacities he served his city and his country with distinction.

In researching this story, I have relied heavily on *The Iconography of Manhattan Island* by I. N. Phelps Stokes, which in its six volumes records on an almost daily basis events that took place in the years from 1783, Evacuation Day, to around 1830 when my story ends. Other sources have included the minutes of the Common Council, the city's governing body; the definitive work of Rocellus S. Guernsey, titled *New York City and Vicinity During the War of 1812–1815*, published in 1889; and the biography of Mary Mapes Dodge, General Mapes's granddaughter.[1] Many others are detailed in the source notes at the end. Most of my research time has been spent in three libraries: the New York Genealogical and Biographical Society Library, the New York Public Library, and the New-York Historical Society Library. I am very grateful to all of them. I have visited several cemeteries in search of gravestones of ancestors, including the Mills family burial ground in Head of the Harbor (near Stony Brook) and the burial ground of the Mattituck Presbyterian Church, both on Long Island. I want to thank Cathy Ball, historian and research librarian of the Smithtown Library for her help with the successful search for the graves of Jonas Mapes and his mother Deliverance Mapes (Mills). I would also like to recognize and thank my two typists, Lauren Bans and Alysha Brown, for the many hours they spent on the manuscript. Finally, I thank my nephew Horace Havemeyer III, who has helped me with the production of this work, as he has with several others.

Harry W. Havemeyer
NOVEMBER 2008

INTRODUCTION

In the early hours of the morning on August 8, 1814, the general had awakened to find an unusual summer rainstorm soaking the New York City area. From his house in lower Manhattan he knew immediately that the weather would make the task planned for that day difficult and that it had best be postponed. Impatient as he was to get started, his experience with volunteer militias persuaded him to wait for more favorable conditions. The time was short, he knew, and the task was vital, but this precise and well-disciplined man had the good judgment to wait 24 hours before starting to build the first of six fortresses that would be needed to protect his city from an expected attack and possible invasion by the mighty British navy, the masters of the sea in that era.

Brigadier General Jonas Mapes at that time stood at the peak of his career. He commanded the Third Brigade of infantry in the First Division of the New York State militia. He had been given the assignment of fortifying the most likely route of a British attack — from Coney Island through Brooklyn to Manhattan, the same used successfully by the British general Howe in 1776 — by erecting a series of six forts with interlocking entrenchments from Wallabout Bay south to Gowanus Creek, all with volunteer militia and citizens called to help. He was well prepared for the task.

At the request of the mayor and the Common Council, General Mapes, a New York City alderman, had gone to Washington, D.C., in early July to meet with President Madison and Secretary of War Armstrong and ask for their support by calling additional militia into federal service and supplying more arms, particularly heavy ordnance. This successful mission was followed in early August by an inspirational speech by the general's close friend Mayor

De Witt Clinton urging all New Yorkers to volunteer for duty and assist in the protection of their city.

It had been more than two years since his country had declared war against Great Britain. Those years saw several naval battles in the Atlantic Ocean and on Lakes Ontario and Erie, two United States invasions into Canada, both of which failed, and the British capture of the U.S. fort in Detroit, Michigan. It was not until Napoleon had fled to Elba in April 1814, ending the British conflict with France, that the British turned their full attention to their former colony. Neither General Mapes nor anyone else in the United States knew how much time there would be before an invasion or a mainland attack would occur. There were rumors and clues, however. U.S. vessels had spotted a large fleet of British Navy ships and transports headed westbound across the ocean, some toward Montreal and Halifax in Canada, and others to their base in Bermuda. More warships were also observed off New York, Long Island, and other Northeastern ports blockading virtually that entire part of the country.

Then on July 14 the news reached New York City that a small force of British marines had landed at the easternmost town along the U.S. coast, Eastport, Maine, and soon had seized the towns of Machias and Bangor before halting at Penobscot Bay. Another British warship had bombarded Saybrook and Stonington, Connecticut, shortly thereafter. General Mapes knew that time was running short and that a British armada could appear off Sandy Hook at any time. He also knew that without the line of forts there would be no chance of stopping the redcoats from pillaging his city. New York, then the largest and most prosperous city in the nation, was certainly the prime target for a devastating raid if not invasion. At forty-six years of age General Mapes felt confident in his leadership and ready to carry out his assignment. On August 9 the weather cleared and the work began.

PART I
On Long Island

CHAPTER ONE

Five Early Settlers

1630–64

This story begins in the first part of the seventeenth century in England and in Holland where two separate struggles had begun that would affect the lives of five families and lead to a decision by each to depart from the land of their birth and undertake a hazardous 3000-mile voyage to a new land only very recently settled, the Massachusetts Bay Colony in America.

The earlier of the two conflicts, a part of the Counter Reformation, was the determined attempt of Philip II of Spain, a fierce Roman Catholic, to gain control of the Protestant Netherlands. This struggle had gone on throughout much of his reign (1555–98) and continued into those of his two successors, with only a short ten-year truce intervening (1610–20), until it ended in 1648 with the Treaty of Westphalia.

The second struggle, which took place in England, was that of Charles I against Parliament, usually called the English Civil War. In addition to the political strife, the king's religious policies caused earlier passions to be aroused in a population that was predominately Protestant, leading to the Great Migration of English Puritans in the 1630s to the Colony of Massachusetts. These Puritans had found the religious demands of the Church of England under its new archbishop of Canterbury, William Laud, appointed by King Charles I in 1633, increasingly rigid and intolerant. Rejecting this intolerance and desiring to maintain their own religious practices, they immigrated to Massachusetts and later to Connecticut and Eastern Long Island, where, ironically, some established theocracies (New Haven and Southold) became as intolerant as those they left behind in England. In fact, many Puritans thought of Charles I as a "closet" Catholic because his queen, Henrietta Maria, was Catholic by birth. In the 1640s both the king and the archbishop would be executed in the aftermath of their defeat in the English Civil War.

This was the background in which five families came to the decision to leave their homes. Of course, they were not alone. More than 20,000 English Protestants came to New England during the decade of 1630 to 1640. It was the largest group of people to move the longest distance in the shortest period in recorded history up to that time.

The surnames of these families were Mapes, Purrier, Gardiner, Hawkins, and Mills, all of English heritage. They emigrated between 1630 and 1635, all from England, except for Gardiner, who departed from Holland, where he had been fighting the Spanish on behalf of the Prince of Orange. All were middle-aged except Mills, who at 45 was considered old, and the youngest Mapes, who at six was still a boy. All except Mapes were married, and the Purriers and Mills had young children. All started their new lives in the Massachusetts Bay Colony governed by John Winthrop, but soon left that theocracy, finally settling in Long Island. The Purriers lived for a short time in Salisbury, Connecticut, and the Gardiners in Saybrook, Connecticut, before moving to Long Island.

THOMAS MAPES

In April 1634 the vessel *Francis* sailed from Ipswich in the English county of Suffolk, bound for Salem in the Massachusetts Bay Colony, founded only four years earlier. It had been just 14 years since *Mayflower* with the first pilgrims had landed at Plymouth to start that colony in the New World. On board *Francis* were two brothers, John Mapes, age 21, and young Thomas, only six years old. It is not known why the brothers made that voyage nor who their parents were. Possibly they were orphans who emigrated with friends or relatives with different surnames.

The Mapes family was well known in the small village of Thelneham, which lies on the river Little Ouse near the Suffolk-Norfolk border. The flat land there was rich farming country, and the residents generally enjoyed prosperous times. The name Mapes can be traced back eight generations to a John Mapes who was born in the early fifteenth century. By 1634 the exodus of Puritans from East Anglia was well under way. Perhaps the brothers left because others were departing and many hands would be needed to build homes in the New World.

After *Francis* arrived safely in Salem, John Mapes must have found work easily and Thomas likely served as his apprentice. Because he later became a professional surveyor, Thomas must have learned that skill while growing up in Salem. It would serve him well in the future, as no land in Long Island, where he would move, had been surveyed at all.

WILLIAM AND ALICE PURRIER

A year after the Mapes brothers arrived in Salem, the ship *Hopewell* departed from London on April 1, 1635, bound for Ipswich, Massachusetts. On board was the family of William Purrier (Purryer in England) from the small village of Olney located in the north of Buckinghamshire near the town of Bedford. William at 36 years of age was well established and could afford to move with his wife Alice, 37, and their three daughters, Mary age seven, Sarah five, and Catherine one and a half. It was said that "He came through the influence of Rev. William Worchester, who had been disposed as rector of that parish [Olney]."[2]

Upon their arrival in Ipswich they built a home that is shown on a 1638 map of the village. It is quite likely that Thomas Mapes came to know the Purrier family, as they lived only 12 miles apart and the communities were very small in the 1630s. Also Thomas was only a year older than their daughter Sarah. Soon the Purriers moved to Salisbury, Connecticut, for a year or two and then in 1640 to Southold, Long Island. William Purrier was said to be the oldest and wealthiest of the early Long Island settlers.

LION AND MARY GARDINER

Lion Gardiner, the same age as Purrier, was also an immigrant in 1635, but with an entirely different background. Born of English parents circa 1599 (possibly in Maidstone, Kent, as that was the name he gave to the area where he settled on Long Island in 1653), Gardiner was educated in Holland in civil and military engineering, which led to his profession as a soldier. He joined the army of the Prince of Orange, Frederick Henry, in the long struggle against the Spanish Netherlands, which was ultimately successful. He was called "a master of the works of fortification," a vital part of warfare at that time when the siege was the tactical form of offense by the Spanish. Sometime prior to 1635 he married Mary Duercant, "a lady of prominent connections" from Woerdam in the Netherlands.

Gardiner himself said, "In the year 1635, I, Lion Gardiner, engineer and master of the works of fortification in the ledgers of the Prince of Orange in the Low Countries, through the persuasion of Mr. John Davenport,* Mr. Hugh Peters, and with some other well-affected Englishmen of Rotterdam, made an agreement with the fore named Mr. Peters for 100 pounds per annum, for four years, to serve the patentees [of Saybrook in the Colony of Connecticut], namely the Lord Say, the Lord Brooks, Sir Arthur Hazilrig, Sir Matthew Bonnington, Esquire Fenwick and the rest of the company — And so I came from Holland to London, and thence to New England."[3] The patentees had promised Gardiner that a proper fort would be built around the new settlement at the mouth of the Connecticut River on Long Island Sound before his arrival there. It was named Saybrook after Lords Say and Brooks.

Thus when the vessel *Bachelor* sailed from the pool of London on August 11, 1635, bound for Boston, three of its passengers were Lion Gardiner, age 36; his wife Mary, age 34; and their maidservant. After a safe arrival they remained only briefly in Boston before heading south, arriving at the new settlement on November 28, just before winter set in. Gardiner was disappointed to find that no fortification had even been started, as promised by the owners. He was faced with the task of "drawing, ordering, and making of a town, forts and fortifications" with 300 men under his command.

To make matters more difficult, the lower Connecticut River Valley was the home of the Pequots, a particularly belligerent tribe of American Indians, noted for kidnapping children of their enemies, both white children and those of other Indian tribes. During Gardiner's early years at Saybrook they continually attacked and harassed the settlement. Once he was seriously wounded but survived. It was not until 1637–38 when the Mohegan and Narragansett tribes combined with the Massachusetts Bay Colony to drive the Pequots out of the Connecticut River Valley that a measure of safety could be found.

During these four years at Saybrook, two children were born to Lion and

---

* The Rev. Davenport was co-pastor of the English church in Amsterdam.

Mary Gardiner: a son, David, in 1636, said to be the first white child born in Connecticut, and a daughter, Mary, in 1638. During these years Gardiner became acquainted with the sachems on Eastern Long Island who wanted protection from the Pequots. "The four brothers, sachems of Montauk, Shinnecock, Shelter Island [Manhanset], and Corchaug, had already agreed in 1637 to pay tribute to the English after the Pequot War."[4] The brother in Shelter Island, Sachem Youghcoe, usually negotiated with the English. The sachem of Montauk, Wyandanch, was younger; later he also signed documents with the English. In 1639 Gardiner purchased from Sachem Youghcoe the large island east of Shelter Island, later to be called Gardiner's Island. When his contract with Saybrook was over he moved his family there after building a house with some laborers from the Saybrook Fort. This newest settlement became the first English settlement in the present state of New York. Their third child, Elizabeth, was born on the island in 1641, the first white child born in Suffolk County, Long Island.

ROBERT AND MARY HAWKINS

During the latter part of April 1635, from the Blackpool section of London, the vessel *Elizabeth and Ann*, commanded by Captain Roger Cooper, sailed for Boston. On board were Robert Hawkynns, age 25, and Marie Hawkynns, age 24 (English spelling of their surnames). Their ages have not been proven, and they may have been stated at less than their real ages, as was the case with other passengers aboard that ship. Although Hawkynns was a common English surname for many generations, nothing is known about Robert and Mary's heritage. Family historian R. C. Hawkins, writing in 1939, speculated that the decision to emigrate was because "the bigoted and overbearing government at home made life there not only intolerable but even insecure, and that in America there was ample room and opportunity for all persecuted creeds."[5] The English Civil War, which formally began in 1642, was already the cause of discord and conflict between those in support of the king and the parliamentarians.

The *Elizabeth and Ann* landed in Charlestown across the harbor from Boston in the early summer of 1635. To the north of where the Charles River emptied into Boston Harbor there was a small hill on top of which Robert chose a site to build a windmill. It became known by the colonists as Windmill Hill. Shortly afterward he built a small house at the bottom of the hill for his family.

The passenger list for *Elizabeth and Ann* listed Hawkins as a husband-man, undoubtedly a farmer who tilled his soil, raised stock, and ran his water-powered gristmill, charging others for that service. He later bought and sold other land, such as his cow commons in 1646. The record shows him owning and selling land in different parts of the Charlestown area, in Southfield, Linefield, and Waterfield. He lived in Southfield in 1638.

In the Massachusetts Bay Colony it was essential to join a church; only churchgoers could become freemen with the right to vote and hold office; it was not enough to be a landowner. Thus on April 17, 1636, Robert was ad-mitted to membership in the First Church of Charlestown (Mary had been admitted earlier that year), and on May 25 he was declared a freeman with all its rights and privileges. The First Church, having been organized in September 1632, was the only church in Charlestown when the Hawkinses joined.

In December 1636 their first child was born, a son, who was baptized Eleazer* in the church records; on October 25, 1639, a second son was bap-tized Zachary or Zachariah; and on April 3, 1642, a third son was baptized Joseph. The choice of biblical names was very common with the early settlers of the country, and these three were used over and over again in the Hawkins family. There is almost no record of Robert Hawkins from 1646 on. His fam-ily story appears lost to history. What is known next is that in 1661 Robert and Mary's son Zachariah, at the age of 22, appeared with several other new settlers in the land records of the seven-year-old village of Setauket on the north coastal shore of Long Island.

GEORGE MILLS

The last of the five immigrants in the story was George Mills, who was born in Yorkshire in the north of England in 1605 and came with his wife to Mas-sachusetts in 1630 or 1631 at the time of the founding of the colony under Governor John Winthrop. Their first son, Samuel, was born in Boston in 1631.

---

* Eleazer was the son of Aaron, the brother of Moses. He was a priest of the Israelites during their 40-year journey through the wilderness to find Canaan, the promised land (see Book of Numbers, Chapters 20 and 21).

Others followed with the names George, Zachariah, Nathaniel, Isaac, and Jonathan. There were possibly girls born as well, but their names have not been recorded.

In 1656 most of the male members of the family, George and his sons, moved from Massachusetts to found a new community in the Dutch-controlled part of Western Long Island. It was known by the Dutch as Rus-dorp (meaning a country village). They were among the first purchasers of land there, and their patents were approved by Governor General Peter Stuyvesant on March 21, 1656. Listed among the first settlers in 1660 were George Mills and his sons Samuel and Nathaniel. In 1664 when the English took control of New Netherland, Rusdorp became Jamaica. George Mills died there in 1694 at age 89, as did his son Samuel in 1726 at age 95. They were a prolific family of great longevity. At his death Samuel and his wife had been married for 68 years, had 16 children (she bore her last at age 51), nine of whom survived him, together with 80 grandchildren and 54 great grandchildren. It was Samuel's son Timothy who would leave Jamaica in 1693 to move to the area near Smith-town, Long Island, to establish his home at Mills Pond.

Connecticut

Fort Saybrook

New Haven

Gardiner's
Island

Southold

Shelter Island

Long Island Sound

Mattituck

East Hampton

Setauket

Long Island

Southampton

Stony Brook

Head of the Harbor

Smithtown

Atlantic Ocean

EASTERN LONG ISLAND AND CONNECTICUT SHORELINE
In Mid 17th Century

CHAPTER TWO

Eastern Long Island

Prior to 1764

Before the English took control of New Netherland in 1664, calling it New York, English-speaking communities on Eastern Long Island at Southold and Southampton (1640), East Hampton (1648), Huntington (1653), and Brookhaven (1655) had supporting, quasi-legal relationships with the two English colonies of Connecticut and New Haven. The latter two were separate until New Haven agreed in 1664 to be part of Connecticut, to which Charles II had recently given a royal charter. Only Southold of the Long Island towns was allied with New Haven. The others chose to ally with Connecticut, which was governed from Hartford on the Connecticut River. In 1664 all of Long Island became part of the new colony of New York under Governor Richard Nicolls.

SOUTHOLD

The North Fork of Long Island's fishtail extends from the mouth of the Peconic River east to Orient Point, a distance of 24 miles. To its north is Long Island Sound and to its south a series of three bays, Peconic, Shelter Island, and Gardiner's Island Bays. The land is flat, the soil is rich from the last glacial deposit, and the climate is mild due to its proximity to the warming currents of the Gulf Stream. Thus the small family farm has been the norm along the North Fork for many generations. Along the bays there are many excellent harbors for boats, making fishing another livelihood for residents.

This was the land chosen by the Reverend John Youngs in 1640 when he arrived with his group of English immigrants searching for a place to settle and build a puritan community. The reverend with his wife and children had departed from the town of Southwold in Suffolk, East Anglia, where he had been born. He was the son of a minister, the Reverend Christopher Youngs, vicar of St. Margaret's, Reydon, a nearby village.

Reverend Youngs and his family sailed in 1637 to Salem, Massachusetts, where on August 14 they were accepted as inhabitants and granted land on which to build. However, they did not remain in Salem for long; in 1639 they moved to join with another new settlement that had been formed along the north side of Long Island Sound at New Haven, by the mouth of the Quinnipiac River.

The New Haven Colony had been started the year before by Theophilus Eaton and his childhood friend, the Reverend John Davenport, a Puritan minister who had left Massachusetts after theological disagreement with Governor John Winthrop and the other leaders of the colony.* Eaton and Davenport believed that Massachusetts had become too lax in the standard of conduct allowed for its people. The Reverend Youngs had sided with the Reverend Davenport and thus with his group had moved to New Haven to join him. However Youngs never intended to remain in New Haven, taking a year to search for a new site across the Sound on Long Island. He wanted to maintain a strong alliance with New Haven because of their compatible beliefs and for the physical protection that settlement could give against Indian attacks.

In 1640 the Reverend Youngs and his group settled on the North Fork of Long Island in a protected location across from Shelter Island. They named the community Southold, after Youngs's home in England—though

---

* John Davenport was educated at Oxford. He became a vicar in London before moving to Holland in 1633, where he founded the Dutch Reformed Church—more sympathetic to his Calvinist Puritanism than the Church of England under Archbishop Laud. He was among those who urged Lion Gardiner to go to Saybrook, Connecticut, in 1635. In 1637 he and Theophilus Eaton, a boyhood friend, went to Boston and then again in 1638 to found a new "strict" theocracy at the mouth of the Quinnipiac River—later called New Haven. Eaton became governor of the separate colony until his death in 1658. Davenport was senior minister of the church until New Haven grudgingly became part of Connecticut in 1664. The Royal Charter given to Connecticut in 1662 included all the territory that had become part of the New Haven, i.e., neighboring towns along the shore and notably Southold in Long Island.

spelled without the "w," which the English never pronounced. They had been helped by the New Haven Colony in negotiating for the land from the Corchaug tribe. At the start Southold was in fact a sub-colony of New Haven, which took title to all of the land on the North Folk in order to exercise control over who could buy land and locate there. This arrangement lasted for nine years until May 30, 1649, when the General Court at New Haven held that residents could take title in their own names. During this "maturing" period Southold agreed that only members of their church "in full communion thereof" had the right to vote or hold any office. This was also the requirement to becoming a "freeman" in Massachusetts. No other Long Island community had such a rule or such a relationship with another settlement. In return Southold received some protection from the Colony of New Haven. Although there was a distance of 30 miles between them, across the often rough Long Island Sound, there was no other group of settlers in 1640 any closer should there be any trouble with the Indians or with the Dutch from New Netherland.

Under the strong leadership of the Rev. Youngs, the village of Southold grew. By 1650, thirty houses had been built, making it the largest community on Eastern Long Island. Among its very first members was the family of William Purrier, arriving in 1640 from Salisbury. William was 41 by then, Alice was 42, and their daughters twelve, ten, and seven. William was a staunch member of the church and a man of wealth. He soon was named a magistrate of the court there. In the years that followed Purrier was chosen to represent Southold at the General Court in New Haven in 1653, 1656, and 1661. In 1662, after New Haven had become part of the Colony of Connecticut, he was designated a "freeman" of Connecticut, a notable honor for a Long Islander. He became a large landholder on the North Fork. After his death the land was inherited by his daughters and their husbands, the Reeve and Mapes families.

In William Purrier's will, written in 1671, he named as beneficiaries his three daughters: Mary, who married Isaac Reeve; Sarah, who married Thomas Mapes; and Martha Osman. His grandson, James Reeve, he named sole executor. He died in 1675 at 76 years of age.

THOMAS AND SARAH MAPES

Thomas Mapes, the young surveyor from Salem, was married to Sarah Purrier in 1650 in her church in Southold.* Thomas was 22 years old and Sarah was 20. They both could look forward to a long, prosperous future and a large family. How and why Mapes came to Southold is not known, but it could have been because of Sarah, whom he likely knew as a very young girl in Ipswich. Southold records show their marriage took place before his first recorded survey in 1652, which would lead one to assume he knew her at an early age before coming to Southold.

Mapes's surveying skills were in great demand. The *History of Mattituck* (a village five miles west of Southold) records that Thomas Mapes, the town surveyor, laid out the 1661 division. He took three lots in the Corchaug section and two lots in the Occabauck section — the Occabauck lots ran from the sound to the bay and were 250 acres each. The Mapes lot east of Elijah Lane was left by Thomas to his son, Jabez. This was a 60-acre farm Thomas had received from William Purrier, his father-in-law.

During Mapes's lifetime much of the land lying west of Southold village to the mouth of the Peconic River was claimed and surveyed. This 15-mile stretch included the villages of Cutchogue, Mattituck, and Aquebogue, together with the richest farmland that had been discovered in all of New England and Long Island. It was a bounty that was not fully appreciated until years later. As has been noted, Thomas claimed large parcels of this land that he would bequeath to his sons.

As the reputation of the young surveyor grew, he was called upon to help another new community 35 miles to the west, known as Setauket. He traveled there in 1655 to survey the land claims of its five original settlers. He also acquired several lots for himself, which he continued to own until at least 1670. This land was farmed and may have been rented or cared for by one of his sons. Thomas was always a resident of Southold, although he did spend time away while surveying.

Thomas's skills combined with the wealth of the Purrier family enabled him to become a leader of the Southold community. He was a justice of the

---

* The original church building in Southold used from 1640 to 1684 was a meetinghouse standing on the south side of the road by the grounds of the old South Cemetery. It was a congregational church then and at a later date joined the Long Island Presbytery.

peace for most of his adult life and was repeatedly elected a constable. Southold historian J. Wickham Case said, "He performed during his life a larger amount of official labor than any one of his early associates."[6]

Sarah and Thomas lived in a house in Southold village on the south side of the main street just west of where the meetinghouse was built and west of where the First Presbyterian Church stands today. Her parents, lived next door. They raised a family of eleven children, not unusual for healthy parents who married young. In his will, which was written in 1686, Thomas divided most of his land among his sons, Thomas, William, Jabez, and Jonathan. Daughters received smaller lots or only sheep and a kettle. His wife and his son Thomas were named his executors. His will was not unusual for that time because women after marriage were required to transfer their land to their husbands.

Thomas Mapes died in 1687 at the age of 59, the year after his will was written. Sarah died ten years later at the age of 67. They surely were buried in the Old Southold Cemetery behind their house. It was the oldest part of the burial ground, known today as God's Acre.

Another resident of Southold was the famous Indian fighter Captain John Underhill. At the age of 45 in 1654 he and his wife settled in the Eastern Long Island community until about 1662, when she died and he remarried after moving to Flushing, New York, and finally to Oyster Bay. Undoubtedly Captain Underhill gave Southold a feeling of security in those early years when it felt threatened by the Dutch.

GARDINER'S ISLAND

Gardiner's Island is located between Long Island's fishtail — the North and the South Forks — Orient Point and Montauk Point. It is about six miles long and four miles wide at its widest point, a fertile land with a good supply of well water. It is a journey of about 18 miles by boat through Plum Gut, with its treacherous tides, to Saybrook, Connecticut, which was the nearest community in 1639 when Gardiner and his family moved there. Although the South Fork is closer, the English settlers did not come to Southampton until 1640 and to East Hampton, the closest to the island, until 1648. Southold is about a 15-mile trip from Gardiner's Island. When the Gardiner family first settled on this remote place they gave it the name Isle of Wight, after the island off the Southern coast of England; it was not until 1683, after Lion's death, that it was officially given his name.

The family lived on their island until 1653, when, feeling the effects of his 50-plus years, he decided to move his wife and two daughters to the newly founded East Hampton. His son David was given the island at age 17 and became the second lord of the manor. Educated in England and married there in 1657, David and his wife returned to the manor and raised a family. It was their second daughter Elizabeth who would later marry James Parshall, a large landowner in Aquebogue on the North Fork.

Lion Gardiner resided in East Hampton until his death in 1665. He was probably the most prominent Englishman to settle in Eastern Long Island, as well as the first.

BROOKHAVEN-SETAUKET

1655–90

The settlement of Brookhaven or Setauket, founded in 1655, was located inside a bay off Long Island Sound on the North Shore of Long Island. It was 35 miles west of Southold and ten miles east of Huntington, which dated from 1653. The bay offered an excellent harbor with protection from storms from all directions, rare along the north coast of eastern Long Island. It was the area known as Port Jefferson Harbor today.

In the spring of 1655, five pioneers arrived from Massachusetts and one, Thomas Mapes, from Southold. Their intention was to acquire land from the Setalcott group of Indians. They were acting as agents for others, with Mapes being their surveyor. They were successful in buying some thirty square miles of land around the site of the landing by the bay. The Indians, who spoke Algonquin, were friendly and helped to clear the land of trees. Soon thereafter settlers arrived from Massachusetts and a few from Southold and Southampton. By 1660–61 about 20 families made up the new community, a smaller one than at Southold. They called their home Ashford at first, then Cromwell Bay, and finally Setauket, after the Indian tribe.

The group agreed upon a town-meeting type of government, with some very strict rules for their protection. No member could sell land to a stranger and no outsider could acquire land without the vote of all. These rules may have slowed the growth of Setauket at its start. They also had a loose association with Southold for protection against attack, fearing the Dutch from New Netherland more than the Indians. Dutch traders were known to operate in Eastern Long Island and had posts there as early as the 1630s. The alliance with Southold ended by 1659 when Setauket leaders applied to the more tolerant Colony of Connecticut at Hartford for an association of support. Two years later Connecticut accepted "the Town of Setaucke on Long Island under its Government upon the terms of Southampton."[7] Three years later the Colony of New York came into being, taking over all of Long Island.

ZACHARIAH AND MARY HAWKINS

On March 29, 1662, Zachariah Hawkins is first mentioned in Setauket land records as holding land in the Old Field — in today's Crane Neck or down toward West Meadow. It is recorded that he built a house in a different location than other townsmen, who at this time used this old neck exclusively for planting.[8] It is also a matter of record that he served as a juror in a magistrate's court in Setauket on December 8, 1663,[9] and that in 1664 he was declared "a freeman" by the court in Hartford, Connecticut (the court of jurisdiction). Thus, it is certain that he had arrived on Long Island by 1661 at the latest. There were so few adult males to perform the necessary tasks that a healthy young man would quickly become a jack-of-all-trades. We do know that he owned and operated a water-driven gristmill. During the first years grain had to be taken across the sound to be ground, but by 1659 a local mill was constructed. The rights to a later mill were granted to Hawkins.

By 1668, Zachariah had become a large landowner and an important figure in the community. He was described as "a man of influence with numerous descendants," a trustee of the village, and an important member of the First Presbyterian Church, the only one in the early days.[10] In 1665 the town leaders had been able to persuade the Reverend Nathaniel Brewster, who had come to visit his sons, to remain and become their first ordained minister. One could say he was overqualified, as he had graduated with the first Harvard class of 1642 and was the grandson of Elder William Brewster, the spiritual leader of the Pilgrims, who sailed on *Mayflower* in 1620 to Plymouth. He was known to preach of more tolerance than could be found in New Haven or

Southold. With only a meetinghouse for Sunday worship, Brewster accepted the task and remained until his death in 1690.

At about the time Zachariah Hawkins arrived, another newcomer, Thomas Biggs, also came to Setauket accompanied by his wife and his daughter, Mary. They had come most likely from Ashford in Kent. Zachariah and Mary were soon married. Their house stood opposite the intersection of what are today Christian and Bay Avenues, a group of trees marking the spot. They had five children: Zachariah, Joseph, Eleazer, Martha, and Hannah, the second and third boys being named for their father's brothers. It was to be the start of a long line of Long Island Hawkins descendants.

MAPES DESCENDANTS
JABEZ TO JOSEPH TO JAMES
1687–1766

Thomas Mapes bequeathed to Jabez, his eighth child, born in 1664, "also one-eighth part of my lot of the meadow and upland on the west side of Mattituck Creek." Several other lots were also mentioned in this bequest, but the land west of Mattituck Creek became Jabez's homestead and would remain in his line of the family from 1687 to after 1800, passing through three generations. It extended from the north of Mapes's Neck on Long Island Sound to Peconic Bay on the south and west from the creek to Mapes's Lane (Cox Neck Road today). About 1707 — but not later than 1715 — Jabez took up residence in a farmhouse he built on Mapes's Neck. It was a substantial heritage.

Jabez Mapes had married Elizabeth Roe, daughter of John Roe of the Setauket family of Roes, who bore ten children. She predeceased her husband, who remarried before his death in 1732. His small gravestone of blue slate in the cemetery adjoining the Mattituck Presbyterian Church survives with the inscription "Here lieth ye body of Jabez Mapes, died January 26, 1732, aged 68 years." The name Jabez comes from an Old Testament figure in the lineage of Judah and means "height" in Hebrew.*

After the death of Jabez the large farm passed to his only son, Joseph (two others had died earlier), who had married Keziah Parshall, the daughter of Captain Israel Parshall and Joanna Swezy. Captain Parshall was a large landowner

---

* I Chronicles 4:9–10.

in Aquebogue, west of Mattituck, where he had acquired lots in 1705 and 1724. He was the son of James and Elizabeth Gardiner Parshall and thus descended through his mother from Lion Gardiner (see Gardiner section).

Joseph Mapes lived on the Mattituck farm from birth to death: 1705 to 1783. He and Keziah had a very large family, although four of their children died in their youth, a not uncommon experience then, and were buried in the Mattituck graveyard. Six survived to adulthood, three sons and three daughters. In Joseph's will written in 1771, twelve years before his death, he gives the use of "my neck of land, on which I now live, to my beloved wife Keziah during her natural life, according to the lease from my son Joseph [his eldest son]." Apparently the family homestead had earlier been given to his son Joseph and leased back. After several other bequests, he directs that the remainder of his estate be divided between his other sons, James and Phineas. Presumably this division included the remainder of his land.

Joseph Mapes's will also directs a disposition of three slaves: a negro man called William and a negro woman called Gense are to be sold, and a negro girl called Hagar is to be given to his daughter Anne. Since early Dutch times in New Netherland, farming families acquired slaves to work in the fields and help in the house, as there was insufficient free labor in the population of settlers. Setauket records show that a slave was owned by Richard Floyd as early as 1672. The practice continued under English rule throughout the eighteenth century and into the nineteenth century until slavery was finally outlawed in New York State in 1827. Some slaves were freed by their owners and worked on the farms as hired help, but others were sold, as was the case with two of Joseph Mapes's slaves. Also, the 1776 census for Southold shows James Mapes (see below) as owning one slave.

Joseph and Keziah's youngest son, James, was born on the farm on April 6, 1746, thirteen years after their elder son, Joseph. A son Phineas and a daughter Joanna had been born in that interval as well as two infants who died. The North Fork of Long Island by that time was no longer in the isolation that existed in Thomas Mapes's day. Many new villages had sprung up in the years since Southold had been settled, but the center of governance remained in the town of Southold. To the west, Riverhead had been founded along the Peconic River, and to the west of that a few small villages had appeared along the North Shore before reaching the town of Brookhaven and its central village of Setauket.

Like the Mapeses, many families were large, and among some there was intensive intermarriage. Finding a spouse was always a concern, and it was quite common for some girls to become spinsters. Boys would leave to find mates elsewhere, but girls could not. Occasionally branches of families would move away altogether; one branch of the Mapes family moved to New Jersey.

The record indicates that on May 14, 1764, 18-year-old James Mapes signed a marriage bond with a young woman from Stony Brook, Long Island. She had the unusual Christian name of Deliverance and was the daughter of Major Eleazer and his wife, Ruth Hawkins. At that time she was 19 and was known to be "a young woman of good family and remarkable force of character." Her family had moved the three or four miles to Stony Brook from Setauket only seven years earlier; her father built a large house there, which in later years became known as the Hawkins-Mount manse (more on this house will follow). Although for the groom to be younger than the bride was unusual then, her parents must have been pleased with the match, as the Mapes name was well known to them and Mattituck was not too far away to visit.

HAWKINS DESCENDANTS, CAPTAIN ELEAZER TO MAJOR ELEAZER TO DELIVERANCE HAWKINS OF SETAUKET AND STONY BROOK, LONG ISLAND

1699–1766

Zachariah Hawkins, founder of the Long Island family, died in Setauket at his house in 1699. He was 60 years old. By that time the community had become well established after a slow start. A church had been organized with a proper minister, a school had been built, and a schoolmaster was found. The English governor of New York, Richard Nicolls, in 1666 required that new patents be issued to landowners after they swore allegiance both to England and to the Province of New York. Taxes were levied and property assessed. The justice of the peace was thenceforth appointed by the governor. In such ways the Long Island towns became less independent than they had been before, but they still retained authority over local matters. The town name of Setauket was changed to Brookhaven, although the village retained its earlier name. It was the only place of any size in the Town of Brookhaven until after the revolution.

Zachariah and Mary Hawkins's third son, Eleazer, was born in 1688 and named for his uncle. In later life he became known as Captain Hawkins, possibly because he was the captain of his own sloop or schooner on the run along the North Shore to eastern or western Long Island or to Connecticut. He married Sarah Owen and they lived in Setauket for most of their lives. They had a large family of eleven children. In 1757, nearing their seventies, they moved to nearby Stony Brook to live their final years with their son and his family. Sarah died there in 1768 and Eleazer in 1772. They were buried in the graveyard of the Presbyterian Church of Setauket, where they had been lifelong members.

Captain Eleazer and Sarah's fourth child, born in 1716 in Setauket, was given his father's name. Joining the New York militia, he rose to the rank of major, afterward being known as Major Hawkins to distinguish him from his father, a captain. It is said that he had known George Washington.

In 1739 young Eleazer married 18-year-old Ruth Mills of Smithtown, Long Island, the daughter of Timothy Mills and his second wife Sarah Longbotham. This marriage joined together two of the oldest families on Long Island. Ruth's grandfather was Samuel Mills of Jamaica, Queens (see section on George Mills), and it was her father who moved to Smithtown in 1693.

The Mills family was very prolific. Timothy had two children with his first wife and eleven with Sarah Longbotham, his second. Ruth, born in 1721, was the ninth of these eleven. Among her siblings were the given names Deliverance and Jonas, which she would use for her own children.

After their marriage in 1739, Eleazer and Ruth Hawkins began their own family of seven children. The first born, named Jonas after Ruth's brother died in infancy; Juliana died in her tenth year; Deliverance, named after Ruth's older sister—who may have died in childbirth in 1727—was born in 1744; Eleazer was born in 1750; Jonas was born in 1752; a second Juliana was born in 1758; and Ann was born in 1762 and died in her sixteenth year. Note that Jonas and Juliana were named after deceased siblings, a common practice of the era.

It was probably the size of their family and the need to care for his aging parents that persuaded Eleazer and Ruth to leave Setauket for Stony Brook. It was only a few miles away and good farmland was available there. The site they found was at the junction of North Country Road and Stony Brook Road only a mile or so east of Mills Pond, where Ruth had grown up. There was an old farmhouse on the corner with good farmland on the north side of the road.

Eleazer set about to greatly enlarge the old house. It eventually would have 18 rooms (eight with fireplaces) gun closets, saddle closets, a third-floor attic, and a spacious kitchen with smoke holes in the ceiling. In 1757 the family moved in: grandparents Eleazer and Sarah; parents Eleazer and Ruth; and the children Deliverance, Eleazer and Jonas, aged thirteen, seven, and five respectively. There was also space for family servants.

It was in this house that Deliverance Hawkins, age 20, signed a marriage bond on May 14, 1764, with James Mapes, an eighteen-year-old lad from Mattituck, Long Island.

Like most people in that era, Major Eleazer was a farmer and as such owned slaves. The 1776 Long Island census listed Eleazer with one negro over the age of 16 and four negroes under the age of 16. They provided labor in the fields and in the house. The life of a typical eighteenth-century Stony Brook farmer was described in a reminiscence by his great grandson. The farmer was Joseph Smith Hawkins, born in 1763, the son of George Hawkins, a younger brother of Major Eleazer and therefore a first cousin of Deliverance and Major Jonas Hawkins. The great grandson was Percy Smith Hawkins, born 1892.

"He used to raise wheat and rye and corn, no small vegetables except in the family garden. There was a big barn on the south side of the house, a hog pit, and many other buildings, which are all gone now. There was I remember six horses and two to twelve cows. I used to, when I was a boy, drive the cows to pasture each morning and back in the evening. The pasture was more than a mile away and I got 75 cents a week." He also remembered that ship captains supplied transportation in their coastal schooners for goods sold in New York City and Connecticut and brought to Stony Brook. Merchants there bought and sold from the schooner captains. "He [Joseph Smith Hawkins] used to make butter and take it to the store and trade it for groceries. Farming was the mainstay of the village, plus the boats that used to bring things in and take things out. My grandfather used to cut and ship cordwood to New York City. The dock at Stony Brook used to be covered with hundreds of cords of wood."[11]

This description of typical Long Island farm life began to change in the nineteenth century, but the Joseph Hawkins family farmed their land until about 1911, when the second Joseph Hawkins passed away.

CHAPTER THREE

James and Deliverance Mapes

1766–83
The Early Years in Southold, Stony Brook, and Setauket

The engagement of Deliverance Hawkins and James Mapes, formalized with a marriage bond, lasted for a period of two years. This arrangement could have been required by the Hawkins family because James was so young at the time and because as the youngest son he did not have the assurance of receiving land from his father. It may have been known that Joseph Mapes had already designated the land for his eldest son, Joseph, in a sale-leaseback arrangement. Younger sons were almost never as favorably treated.

However, at the end of the two-year waiting period, on June 20, 1766, the couple was formally married and went to live together on the Mapes farm in Mattituck. It is not known if they lived with James's father and mother or in their own house on the land. Very soon thereafter, in late 1766 or early 1767, their first child, a son, was born and named after both father and mother: James Hawkins Mapes. Apparently childbearing was not difficult for Deliverance, as she was soon pregnant again. On September 6, 1768, a second son was born, whom they named Jonas Mapes after Deliverance's brother. The two young sons were taken to be baptized together on November 22, 1769, by Reverend Benjamin Goldsmith, pastor at the parish of Aquebogue, a Congregational Church.

The name Jonas is almost never seen today. In fact it was rarely used in the eighteenth century, when biblical names were very common. On Long Island one can examine the genealogy of family after family and not find the name Jonas. The name itself is a derivation of the Latin for the English Jonah, the book of the Bible. Jonah was a minor prophet who was swallowed by a whale.

In Long Island history the earliest immigrants with the name Jonas appear to be Jonas Wood and Jonas Halstead in the settlement of Hempstead in 1644. They both came from the hamlet of Halifax in Yorkshire, England, where it is said the name was commonplace.[12] The Halstead family intermarried with the Mills family who moved to Smithtown, and the latter intermarried with the Hawkins family. Both used Jonas in naming their offspring.

A third child was born to James and Deliverance in 1772, a daughter named Joannah. With her birth their family was complete as far as is known. This does seems strange, as Deliverance was not yet 30 years old and was in good health.

By 1776 the family appeared to be living in their own home on their land in Mattituck. The Suffolk County census that year identified James Mapes, head of family, with a wife and children, not named, and one negro above 15 years of age, most likely a slave. James was also noted in town records as a constable, a position appointed by the Southold town council. It showed that he had the respect of the town fathers.

In September 1776, James was 30 years old, Deliverance was 32, and their children were ten, eight, and four. It was the beginning of a difficult period for them, as it was for all Long Islanders, when their land was occupied by British troops for almost eight years. No other parts of the American colonies were occupied for as long as New York City and Long Island. Prior to the invasion of Brooklyn and General Washington's defeat at the Battle of Long Island, the revolutionary fervor that was shown in Massachusetts and Virginia did not extend to eastern Long Island, where the several isolated communities were far removed from the events in Boston that so outraged its citizens. Long Islanders were generally loyal to King George III, and the majority were considered loyalists throughout much of the eight years of occupation. There were some notable patriots however, and many families were split in their feelings, which caused tensions among them. For example, General William Floyd of Mastic signed the Declaration of Independence, while his cousin Colonel Richard Floyd joined the Tories.

No matter what their feelings, all suffered economically, as Long Island farmers were expected to feed the troops occupying both Long Island and

New York City, leaving much less for the local population. This in itself caused hardship. Further disruption was caused by British troops in places where they were garrisoned such as Setauket. "[It] became a garrison town. The British converted the Presbyterian Church into a fort, and stationed more than 250 troops there. Many of these were quartered in private homes in the village.... Most of the fighting in the Setauket area was in the nature of lightening raids, staged by whaleboatmen and guerilla bands [from Long Island Sound]."[13]

On one matter the villages of the North Shore were in agreement with the New England patriots: British trade restrictions were unjust. Widespread smuggling through North Shore harbors continued throughout the occupation in spite of the soldiers' effort to stop it. Boats would slip into Setauket and Mattituck harbors at night, laden with molasses, rum, sugar, cocoa, and Spanish gold. They would leave with whale oil, tallow, beef, pork, fish, and grain. Many Long Island fortunes were made in this trade.

From 1779 to 1781, Setauket became the focal point for the Culper spy ring that greatly aided the patriot cause, resulting in the unveiling of Benedict Arnold as a traitor and the capture of British major John André. The ring consisted of Robert Townsend, alias Culper Jr.; Abraham Woodhull, alias Culper Sr.; Major Benjamin Tallmadge,* alias John Bolton; Caleb Brewster, boatman; Austin Roe, principal messenger; and Jonas Hawkins, occasional messenger. All were from Setauket, Stony Brook, or Oyster Bay. Townsend in New York City would collect information about British troop movements and write letters in code with disappearing ink. These were carried by Roe and Hawkins to Woodhull in Setauket over 55 miles by road. From Woodhull they were taken by Brewster in his whaleboat to the Connecticut shore where Major Tallmadge had posted dragoons every 15 miles to pick them up and see that they were delivered to General Washington. Austin Roe became so expert at avoiding capture on his Long Island round trips to New York that he eclipsed Hawkins and the other messengers. He was never caught. In August 1779, Jonas Hawkins carried Townsend's letter, but fearing capture, he destroyed it before reaching Woodhull in Setauket. He was not as bold as Roe, and capture with the letter would have meant certain death.[14]

A New York State militia was formally authorized by the state convention

---

* Major Tallmadge was a veteran of the Battle of Long Island in August 1776.

in 1777 held in Kingston on the Hudson River. Led by John Jay, Gouverneur Morris, and Peter Livingston, this convention adopted the first New York State Constitution. George Clinton was elected governor on July 9 and thus became commander of the state militia. Suffolk County established its first regiment with more commissioned officers from the Setauket area, such as Major Tallmadge, than any other on Long Island. Deliverance Hawkins Mapes's father, Major Eleazer Hawkins, and later her brother Major Jonas Hawkins both held commissions in the state militia.*

By the end of the occupation, feelings against Tory sympathizers grew to the boiling point. The patriots had suffered too much and for too long. Tory loyalists still in office were voted out and their property was confiscated. Most fled to Nova Scotia or to England when the British troops left in November 1783.

Southold suffered as well. A British garrison was located on a twenty-acre camp lot next to the parsonage and athletic grounds of the church in the neighboring Mattituck. The homestead of Deacon Thomas Reeve was used as headquarters of the officers, many of whom were quartered in houses of the people. The farmers were required to feed this garrison of occupying troops. The Mattituck church minister Rev. John Davenport, a staunch patriot, fled to Connecticut in 1776, leaving no pastor to serve the people for the entire occupation. There was no meeting of the Suffolk County Presbytery from October 31, 1775, to April 4, 1784, almost 10 years. By 1780 British troops began to withdraw from the North Fork and patriots began to return home, but it was not until after Evacuation Day, November 25, 1783, that any Long Islanders could feel safe. Then they were further embittered by their own state when New York in 1784 put a heavy tax upon them because of their failure to bear a share of the expenses of the war. It seemed to them like an act of injustice.

During the war years the two Mapes sons grew from boys to young adults. By 1783 they were 17 and 15 years old and counted on heavily to work the family farm. They must have watched events from afar and have been told about the role of their Uncle Jonas, who helped to defeat the "redcoats." This

---

* In the first post-occupation listing of military officers in the state militia, the Council of Appointments records Jonas Hawkins as Captain No. 1 under Lt. Colonel Jeffrey Smith, Commandant of the Suffolk County regiment. In 1787 Hawkins was promoted to Major No. 2 under Lt. Colonel David Pierson. Hawkins was then 35 years old. He resigned in 1797.

clearly made an impression on Jonas Mapes, the younger of the two, who likely looked upon his uncle and namesake as a role model. His later military career can be traced to this source.

The year 1783 was also a turning point for the Mapes family, particularly for Deliverance and her children. The year began with the death in January of James's father, Joseph, patriarch of the family, at the age of 78. He had lost his wife, Keziah, the year before, following a marriage of 55 years. With his death his eldest son, Joseph, became the head of the family. Even as the father was dying that January, it was apparent that his son James was ill and that it was necessary for him to write a will. That will, a very short one, was signed on February 5, saying "I, James Mapes, of Southold [town of registry] in ye County of Suffolk, being sick and weak in body . . . I leave to my well beloved wife Deliverance, all my lands, buildings, and improvements, together with all my real and personal estate, while my widow." As the children were all minors at that time they received nothing. However, in the event that Deliverance remarried, she would only receive 100 pounds, a horse, and a riding chair; in that case all his estate would be equally divided among his two sons and daughter. He named his wife and brother-in-law Joseph (Jonas)* Hawkins executors, rather than either of his own brothers Joseph or Phineas, which could have been due to his knowledge that she would have to rely more heavily upon Joseph (Jonas) and the Hawkins family.

Ten days after signing his will James Mapes died; he was not yet 37 years old. Deliverance, was 38, with three children ranging in age from 11 to 16. Like his mother, Keziah (d. 1782), and his father, Joseph (d. 1783), James most likely was buried on family property in Mattituck. There was no listing of their names in either of the two burial grounds by the Reverend Benjamin Goldsmith, the minister in charge of both the Mattituck and Jamesport (Aquebogue) parishes in those two years.[15] The sudden, unexpected death of her husband left Deliverance dependent to a large degree on his family, particularly his brothers Joseph and, to a lesser degree, Phineas.

---

* There is no record that Deliverance Hawkins Mapes had a brother named Joseph. She did have a brother Jonas Hawkins, who lived in the Stony Brook Manse with his family in 1783. She also had a first cousin named Joseph Smith Hawkins who lived in Stony Brook in the village near Hawkins Road. Both were farmers. Jonas was 31 years old in 1783 and Joseph was 20 that year she became a widow. I suspect that James Mapes named his brother-in-law Jonas Hawkins as executor in his will and that a typist mistakenly changed Jonas to Joseph when copying a longhand document in which the Christian name Jonas was either unfamiliar or illegible.

Although she did inherit her husband's land and other assets, gaining a livelihood and providing for her children from her inheritance would have been very hard without help from her brothers-in-law. It is known that Phineas had a family of his own and in fact named a daughter Deliverance (baptized 1771), which would indicate that he was friendly. But from Joseph, the new patriarch, it was doubtful that she received any help. In any event her sons had to work full-time to maintain the farm. Without them she could not manage the property she inherited, and remarriage was out of the question. No man would marry a widow with three children when the children would eventually own all the property. The years following James's death must have been a great struggle for Deliverance. Could she get help from her brother, Jonas Hawkins, who occupied the big house of their father in Stony Brook?

It is not certain how long Deliverance remained in Mattituck after James's death. As all of her assets were in land, she would have to arrange to sell them should she decide to move. That process could have taken time, particularly if she had a difficult relationship with Joseph Mapes. Surely her young sons would not stay on the farm any longer than necessary to help their mother and sister. They must have been restless to start a different life.

By 1788 there is some evidence that the family had moved. It is recorded that her eldest son had married Mary Ann Janes by then, and their children were subsequently born in the west. Also some sources state that her son Jonas had left for New York City by then. He would have been 20 years old that year. With only her daughter to look after, it is likely that Deliverance returned to the Hawkins house in Stony Brook where both her aging parents still lived with her brother Jonas and his family.

Jonas had been born in 1752, eight years after Deliverance. In 1775 he married Ruth Mills, the daughter of Jonathan and Ruth Mills, who confusingly had the same maiden name as his mother. They would have a family of nine children, some of whom lived to adulthood. Like his father, Jonas joined the state militia, later to become a major. It was said he was a trusted friend of General Washington and a messenger in the Setauket spy ring (see above).[16] He was also a farmer like his father; he would take over the Hawkins farm and with his large family live in the manse on Stony Brook Road. In 1791 after Major Eleazer's death the homestead was turned over to Jonas, who had been living there since boyhood. Along with his own family were his elderly mother, Ruth, and probably his older sister, Deliverance Mapes, with her daughter Joannah.

Although the manse was full again, change was soon to come. In 1801 Ruth Mills Hawkins died at age 79, and in the same year Joannah Mapes left to marry Jonas Smith. Micah Hawkins left to go to New York City to find a new life, and Julia left to marry Thomas S. Mount of Setauket. Micah would later meet up with his cousin Jonas Mapes in the city, and Julia would come home again as a widow.

Jonas Hawkins died in 1817 at the age of 65. But three years earlier, after the death of her husband, Thomas Mount, Julia, his 32-year-old widow, came back with her five children to live with their grandparents in the manse. With the arrival of the Mount children in 1814 the house began to look like an art studio. Three sons became artists, and the youngest son, William Sidney Mount, achieved great acclaim in later life. The manse became known as the Hawkins-Mount House and today is a national landmark.

PART II

In New York City

CHAPTER FOUR

Postwar New York City

1783–1800

The British troops left New York City in tatters when they departed on November 25, 1783. It came to be called Evacuation Day. At the outset of their occupation, the Great Fire of 1776 had destroyed a quarter of the city, from Whitehall up to the west side, including Trinity Church to Barclay Street, where King's College was located. A second fire in August 1778 was followed by an explosion of gunpowder aboard an ordnance ship in the East River, both of which damaged more property as well as some east-side wharves. Nothing had been done to rebuild the city during the seven years of British occupation. Although New York's population had increased for a short time during this period because loyalists from around the colonies fled to the capital of Tory America, they departed in 1783 for Nova Scotia and England, and so the population declined again to only 12,000, smaller than it had been for several decades. It was described then as "a most dirty, desolate, and wretched place." The city extended north from the tip of Manhattan to wooden palisades that the British had built from the North River to the East River along Chambers Street (today's name). Near the north wall stood the infamous Bridewell Prison (west of City Hall today), where patriot prisoners-of-war had been held as well as on ships moored across the East River in Wallabout Bay. The job of rebuilding did not take place right away. One New Yorker returning in 1789 found the city "a neglected place, built chiefly of wood, and in a state of prostration and decay . . . there was silence and inactivity everywhere."[17]

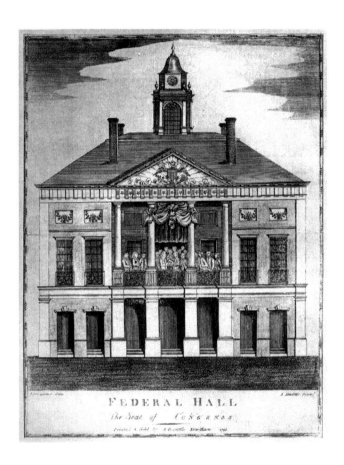

FEDERAL HALL
The Seat of Congress

FEDERAL HALL, THE SEAT OF CONGRESS
Engraved by A. Doolittle, New Haven, CT, 1790. Line engraving. Date depicted: April 30, 1789.
Washington's inauguration, the year after Jonas Mapes moved to New York City.
He was 21 years old at that historic moment.

VIEW OF BROAD STREET AND
FEDERAL HALL ON WALL STREET

A watercolor drawing by John Joseph Holland, 1797. The steeple on the left is that of St. Paul's.
The only contemporary view of the upper end of Broad Street in the 18th century.

Broadway, destroyed in the 1776 fire, was still in ruins. Virtually the entire merchant class, being Tories, had left in 1783 with the British forces, and a new group of merchants were only slowly getting started.

In spite of the observation of the New Yorker quoted above, it can be argued that a recovery had started by 1785. It was in that year that the Congress of the United States met in Federal Hall on Wall Street at the head of Broad Street and would do so until 1790. New York had become the nation's capital.

Although rebuilding was slow to begin, there were other signs of revival in the city. King's College on Barclay Street, which had not been destroyed in the 1776 fire, opened in 1784 but with a new name: Columbia College. In this period a few students were being instructed by even fewer faculty members, but a start had been made. Also in 1784, Alexander Hamilton, soon to be New York's most influential citizen, founded the Bank of New York on Pearl Street, the most commercial street near the East River wharves. The bank became vital to New York's revival. Mayor James Duane (1784–1789) and five commissioners were appointed to supervise the rebuilding of the burned-out west side. Fort George was to be leveled in 1788 to make way for a presidential mansion, which became the residence of the state governor after the federal government moved.

On April 30, 1789, George Washington, having been unanimously elected president of the United States, was inaugurated on the upper balcony of Federal Hall. Extensive alterations had been made on the old colonial City Hall after designs by Major Charles L'Enfant. The enlarged and remodeled building became Federal Hall, a more fitting name for the capitol of the new nation. However, neither President Washington nor most members of Congress liked New York City, and in August 1790 the capital was moved to the nation's largest city, Philadelphia.

The nation's first census, taken in 1790, showed Philadelphia with a population of 42,520, while New York's was 33,131. The latter had tripled in size since Evacuation Day seven years before and was catching up on its rival to the south. New York's census then also showed 3,470 African Americans, of whom 2,369 were slaves. There were 2,500 German immigrants and 5,000 Irish immigrants, the latter group growing most rapidly after the English. The pace of Irish immigration had already become a concern to the merchant class in the city, which was largely of English origin. They felt their livelihood was threatened and that they had no representation among city leaders who were primarily from the gentry.

Thus in 1786 a group of tradesmen came together to form an organization to promote their interests. They called themselves the Society of Saint Tammany or Columbian Order, Tammany being a legendary Indian chief. The society at first was a patriotic, fraternal organization to counterbalance the hereditary, aristocratic Society of the Cincinnati, which was made up of officers of the Continental army and their sons. The Society of Saint Tammany did however soon become political, bitterly opposing the election of Irish immigrants to public office on the ground that they were Roman Catholic. They worked closely with the General Society of Mechanics and Tradesmen to represent their common interests.

Saint Tammany was led by twelve sachems (leaders) under a grand sachem. William Mooney, who had been an enlisted man in the Revolutionary Army, was the first grand sachem. One of the twelve sachems was the leather merchant James Tylee, who had been imprisoned by the British during the war in Bridewell Prison. Tylee's family were early settlers in Connecticut. He was a fierce patriot, a leader of the trade union movement in the 1790s and elected president of the General Society of Mechanics and Tradesmen in 1798. It was a strict rule that sachems must be native-born citizens, meaning white males who were not Roman Catholic. It was not until after 1800 that the Society of Saint Tammany, under the leadership of Aaron Burr, became known as Tammany Hall and became outwardly political and pro-Irish.

The rebuilding of New York City accelerated after 1789. Streets were laid out and by 1796 some were graded north to Houston Street. Most important was the decision of the Common Council to construct two outer streets, South Street on the East River side and West Street on the Hudson River side. They were 70 feet wide, separating wharves from any building. Existing water lots were condemned, and slips and boat basins built by the Dutch and the English were filled in. In Manhattan, riparian rights were owned by the city rather than by private interests. One of those slips filled in along the East River was Old Slip built by the Dutch. Craftsmen were located in that area, one of whom in 1789 was the merchant tailor John Waldron at number 18 Old Slip. He was from one of the earliest families to settle in New Amsterdam, in 1654. His address was renumbered 3 Old Slip in 1794 when all buildings in the city were required to have numbers for the city directory. He remained there until his death in 1798. Development of the waterfront was particularly important to the future of New York as a major port.

Parallel to the East River the principal streets were South Street (from 1796), Front Street, Water Street (formerly Queen Street), and Pearl Street. As the city expanded, these streets were extended northeast. Pearl Street became the center for the wholesale dry goods trade, which included boot makers, tailors, jewelers, and hairdressers. Water, Front, and South Streets were lined with shops and grocery warehouses. The Fly Market, the city's oldest, at the foot of Maiden Lane, had been improved with three market houses for meat, country produce, and fish. Later the fish market moved to the end of Fulton Street.

Among the graded streets running north was Broadway, the fashionable residential avenue on which stood elegant shops in the retail, dry goods trade. On Broadway at the end of Wall Street, Trinity Church rebuilt in 1791 the structure that had burned in 1776. St. Paul's Church stood slightly to the north. Broadway continued up the center of Manhattan over an arched bridge across Collect Pond and reached Houston Street by 1796.

Along the Hudson River on the west side, Greenwich Street was extended north from the Battery to Greenwich Village, where Newgate, the state prison, was built. Development of wharves there proceeded at a slower pace.

Integral to Manhattan's early expansion after the war was the disposition of the DeLancey Farms in the 1780s. This huge piece of property, as large as all of developed Manhattan from the Battery to today's City Hall, was located from King's Bridge Road on the west to the East River, and from Corlear's Hook (where the East River turns sharply north) to Houston Street. It had been owned by New York's most affluent and famous loyalist, Oliver DeLancey, who fled to Nova Scotia before Evacuation Day in 1783. His farms were taken over by the state and subsequently purchased by leading patriot families such as Livingston, Delameter, Fish, Beekman, Roosevelt, and many others. There were in total 175 purchasers, including 69 self-designated "gentlemen," merchants, and lawyers. DeLancey's mansion at Pearl and Broad Streets became Fraunces Tavern.

An important part of commercial life of the revived city was the coffee house, not to be confused with the tavern, which was also prevalent. Coffee houses were places of business for merchants of all descriptions. They were

· PARVÆ · RES ·

CONCORDIA

CRESCUNT.

I Certify and declare that the Armorial Bearings above depicted do of
right belong and appertain to the Company of Merchant Taylors and
agree with the original grant made by Robert Cooke, Clarenceux, and
that they are recorded in the College of Arms, London.

College of Arms
   24 May 1881

SIGNED Albert S Woods
               Garter

THE COAT OF ARMS OF THE
WORSHIPFUL COMPANY OF MERCHANT TAYLORS

First granted in England in 1481. General Mapes was a member of the tailor's guild in New York.

where trading took place, an early form of the Merchants Exchange and the Stock Exchange together. The most famous was the Tontine Coffee House, which opened in 1793 on the northwest corner of Wall and Water Streets, one block from the East River wharves in the heart of the most commercial part of Manhattan. Each subscriber put up $200 to become a member of the coffee house, which became a profitable investment for many. Some securities brokers began trading there in 1793.

Also revived were the craft guilds. These were like the merchant guilds began in Europe in the late Middle Ages for the purpose of regulating trade and commerce. Their function was monopolistic, controlling who could trade in a commodity or craft a product. They restricted entry by adopting strict rules of apprenticeship that required a passage of a final test to become a master of the craft. There were guilds for all trades and crafts in New York from early English days, which were offshoots of the London livery companies. One of these was the Merchant Taylors' Guild; another was the Leathersellers' Guild (also known as the Tanners' Guild). In London these guilds often maintained independent schools that provided a classical education for the trainees before they graduated to become masters of their craft.*

Fortunes were made and lost in the history of New York City, but in those very early years when the city was booming, only a few merchants began to accumulate large amounts of capital. One of these was a young man from Germany who settled in New York in 1784, only a year after Evacuation Day. By 1794 he had become America's most important merchant trader with a home on Broadway, the most exclusive residential address. For John Jacob Astor, his greatest successes still lay ahead.

Dutch New Amsterdam was famous for the large number of taverns that were available in such a small area south of Wall Street where the village lay. In 1653 there existed more than 100, serving a population of fewer than 10,000, or one for every 100 men, women, and children—that meant as children and women never entered taverns, there was a tavern for every twenty

---

* The Merchant Taylors' Company in London, which ranks sixth or seventh (the number is in dispute) in precedence out of over 90 guilds, can be traced back to 1327, when it received a charter from Edward III. It founded the Merchant Taylors' school in 1561 and maintains a great hall on the same site at 30 Threadneedle Street, where it was first located in 1345. It was gutted in the great fire of 1666 and badly damaged by bombs in 1940, but has been rebuilt and is used today to host private occasions to raise money for its school, which now is in Middlesex, having moved outside the city in 1933.

men. Beer, not water, was the beverage of choice. That tradition continued down the centuries, and in the 1790s there were many taverns in New York offering rooms for guests, banquets, and political meetings as well as food and drink. The King's Head on Pearl Street was notable in the commercial district. The first of New York's grand hotels, the City Hotel, opened in 1794 and was located on lower Broadway at Cedar Street, with fashionable shops on the ground floor opening onto the street. Four years later the Park Theater began to offer plays from the stage of an auditorium that could seat 2,400. It was located on Chatham Street (Park Row today) near the park south of where City Hall would later stand.

From Evacuation Day New York State was divided politically between Federalists and Republicans, who united only to elect George Washington president in 1789. In all other elections and on most issues they differed sharply. So great was the division that the New York State convention was not able to ratify the new federal constitution for a whole year, and then only by a margin of three, 30 to 27 votes. It was the eleventh of thirteen states to do so. Strong opposition upstate led by Governor George Clinton feared that too much authority had been given to the central government. Only an agreement that a bill of rights would be added (which happened in 1790) permitted ratification at all in New York.

In 1789 the two most important Federalists in New York were Alexander Hamilton and John Jay. Hamilton was President Washington's secretary of the treasury. He had been the principal author of the Federalist Papers, responsible for building a strong, viable federal government. He was head of the party nationally as well as in New York State. Jay, ten years older than Hamilton, was appointed chief justice of the Supreme Court, after having successfully negotiated with Great Britain the treaty under which the two nations would conduct their affairs during the first years of American independence.

In the Republican Party Governor George Clinton was the dominant figure in New York State, always opposing Hamilton on almost every matter. Clinton came from the Hudson Valley, was close to farmers, and held views similar to those of Thomas Jefferson. Allied with Clinton, some of the time at least, was Aaron Burr from New York City, who would later lead Tammany Hall.

At the local level, political structure in the city remained much the same as it had been under British rule since 1683, when Governor Dongan had installed the system of wards with a common council and chaired by a mayor, as in London. The common council decided local matters, but the governor, by appointing both the mayor and the aldermen, controlled the affairs of the city.*

However, the New York State Constitution of 1777, by which the city was governed after Evacuation Day, provided that aldermen would be elected by the people of the wards from which they came, and that a council of appointment, consisting of the governor and a few state senators, would appoint the mayor. This constitutional provision remained in effect until 1821, when it was revised again (more about this will follow).

In 1791 the state legislature created seven newly defined wards of similar size, numbered one through seven, which replaced the north, east, south, and west wards used by the British. Each of the seven wards elected one alderman and one assistant. These fourteen men, with the addition of the mayor and a recorder, made up the Common Council. They exercised authority over all local matters and guided the growth of the city. As the city expanded, more wards were created.

Although seemingly democratic, in fact local government was much less so because the right to vote was so restricted. The Anti-Loyalist Act of 1784 had barred from voting or holding office all persons who were office-holders under British rule, served in the British Army, abandoned the state during the war, or had joined the British. However, thanks to Hamilton, the section preventing those who fled the city from voting was repealed two years later. Suspected Tories who did return were not allowed to own property and thus could not vote. The voting franchise was limited in the 1777 Constitution to freeholders owning property worth at least twenty pounds, (fifty dollars) and to residents of the city admitted as freemen. In 1790 this group amounted to only 1,800 people, 28 percent of the adult white males from the merchant class with strong Federalist leanings.

During the 1790s as the city's population grew from 33,000 to 60,000 people, the first of many health crises occurred. In the summer of 1795 many young and old began to come down with a sickness from which they quite quickly died. No one knew the reason for these mysterious deaths. Living conditions were overcrowded and unsanitary and the drinking water was very poor, but that had been the case for many years in the past. Affluent New

---

* An alderman was an elder man or senior counselor.

Yorkers moved north to country homes or to Long Island to escape the epidemic, but for most it continued throughout the summer into the fall. Before the arrival of cold weather brought an end to the crisis, 732 people had died. The summers of 1796 and 1797 were free of the epidemic but in 1798 it occurred again, with more than 1,300 reported deaths. The mystery was not positively identified until a century later when the mosquito was found to be the carrier of a disease called yellow fever because its victims turned "the color of unpolished brass" before dying.[18] Yellow fever plagues occurred regularly in New York and other cities throughout the nineteenth century.

It was into this bustling, growing city filled with a jumble of old buildings and very few new ones that twenty-year-old Jonas Mapes arrived in 1788 to begin a new life far away from his family home.

CHAPTER FIVE

Jonas Mapes in New York
1788–1807

It must have taken courage and an adventuresome spirit to move alone from the security of family to what was thought of as a big city by a Long Island farm boy. It is not known if Jonas had any personal contacts except possibly through the militia, which he may have joined while still in Stony Brook. Through his uncle Jonas Hawkins, a major in the state militia, he could have been provided an introduction to the New York City militia in its infancy.

Sometime prior to 1794 he registered for duty and began his training, and on October 2 of that year, was commissioned to the officer ranks as ensign in Lieutenant Colonel James M. Hughes's Fifth Regiment of the Brigade of Militia of the City and County of New York. Only a year later he was promoted to first lieutenant (December 7, 1795) and three years after became a captain of the same regiment. This rapid rise in rank to captain in less than ten years speaks to his military aptitude during a peaceful time, though also to his political connections.

The New York State militia was never a full-time occupation for anyone, although it did have periodic drilling exercises to prepare for the call to duty.* New York State historian Alexander C. Flick described it thus:

The militia system as it existed up to the outbreak of the War of 1812 was so indefinite, even chaotic, that it scarcely merited the designa-

---

* In 1862 New York State changed the name of its militia to National Guard, State of New York.

tion of "system" at all. There was, for instance, no exact definition of
the duties and responsibilities of the militia. It might be called out by
the president, in which event the federal treasury bore the cost of
service. It might be called into service by the governor acting under
state law and at state expense. It might also be summoned by militia
officers of divisional, brigade, or regimental rank in case of invasion.
There was, moreover, no recognized procedure in compelling militiamen to respond to summonses calling them out. The terms of service
were short, six months being the maximum period for continuous
service. Theoretically, militiamen were to provide their own muskets
or rifles, but in reality many of them did not, or could not, do so. During parade periods, it was not unusual for one regiment to borrow
arms from another, and because of laxity in regulations, arms supplied
by the state often could not be recovered. Few of the higher militia
officers had any extensive knowledge of, or experience in, military affairs, and there was wide acceptance of the idea that militiamen could
not be ordered out of the United States.[19]

The militia, however, was under the control of the governor and the state legislature and was the direct responsibility of the adjutant general of the state.
Awarding commissions and promotions was political. The governor of New
York — George Clinton from 1777 to 1795 — and the council of appointments looked carefully at awarding commissions in the militia. It is uncertain
when Jonas Mapes met his father-in-law to be, James Tylee. A leather merchant and a sachem of the Tammany Society, Tylee was well known to the
governor. He could have also helped the military career of the young man who
would soon marry his daughter.

In addition to joining the militia, Jonas Mapes needed to establish himself in a trade or craft to earn a livelihood, to marry and raise a family. With a
modest education at best and no sponsor, Columbia College was out of the
question. He needed to find a master tradesman under whom he could apprentice. Tylee was one of these, but he did not turn to him. As it is known
that by 1794 Mapes was listed as a tailor at 335 Pearl Street* and that years
later he would take into his firm young Victor Waldron as an apprentice, it is

---

* See New York Directory

THE ROBERTS PLAN OF NEW YORK

Published in 1797 by B. Taylor after J. Roberts. Line Engraving. At the time of Mapes's marriage to Elizabeth Tylee, his tailor's shop was at 335 Pearl Street near the East River.

likely that he began his own apprenticeship with Victor's father, the merchant tailor John Waldron at 18 Old Slip. It was the city's oldest slip, built in Dutch times on the East River side of Manhattan. Waldron was also a sachem of Tammany with Tylee and thus an acquaintance of his. Many of the trade and craft guilds were located close to wharves where ships from abroad docked. It was a short apprenticeship for Jonas, but by the age of 26 he was fully established with a business of his own and with the rank of ensign in the militia. He could then consider marriage.

On October 12, 1796, Jonas Mapes married Elizabeth Tylee, the daughter of James. Elizabeth was 19 that year, almost ten years younger than her husband. She had been born in Manhattan when it had been under British control and must have suffered along with her mother and brothers while her father had been held in Bridewell Prison. It was reported that "when smallpox was daily thinning out the prisoners in the manner of a later Andersonville, Mrs. Tylee conveyed into the prison supplies of vaccine, with instructions as to its proper use, concealed in loaves of bread which she furnished to her husband and friends."[20]

Elizabeth's father, a leather merchant after the occupation ended, became a leader in the growing community of tradesmen that were needed as the population grew. In addition to being a sachem of the Tammany Society he was a founder of the General Society of Mechanics and Tradesmen and later its vice president and president. This was an important position in the city. Tylee represented the leather trade and was designated an inspector of leather by the Common Council.

The need for leather goods was large those days because not only did people require leather coats and boots, but horses needed saddles and reins. The leather tanneries required a source of pure water and the bark of hemlock trees, which when crushed was the best source of tannin to give strength to animal hides. Tanning was a dirty and smelly process near which no one would live. In Manhattan they were located near Collect Pond in an area known as "The Swamp." Fresh water came from the pond and hemlock bark from the north part of Manhattan. By 1810 the tanneries were forced to move to the Catskills and Collect Pond was filled in and built over.

After their marriage Jonas and Elizabeth most likely lived over the tailor's shop at 335 Pearl Street. Located between Peck's Slip and Dover Street, it was within a block of where the ferry from Brooklyn landed, a favorable location for passengers needing clothing. (Before the advent of the department store, the merchant tailor would clothe both men and women when they needed apparel not made at home.) It was also near the wharves that were being built during the entire time that Mapes remained there. Ships bringing wool and cotton cloth from England or France docked nearby. At that time his father-in-law had his leather shop at 83 Chatham Street, only a few blocks inland and closer to Collect Pond.

In 1798 Jonas Mapes moved his tailor shop to 245 Water Street, a block nearer to the East River between Peck's Slip and Beekman Street. Perhaps a larger space was required, for in that year his former master John Waldron died (possibly of yellow fever in the epidemic that year) and as a result Jonas received the benefit of some of his customers, as Peck's Slip and Old Slip were only ten blocks apart.

John Waldron was only 47 when he died. His second wife Aletta, age 44, died in the same year, leaving their youngest son, Victor B. Waldron, an orphan only a year old. John Waldron had been the father of five children with his first wife and eight with Aletta, born between 1785 and 1797, so any of the older siblings could have raised Victor, who later became an apprentice tailor under Jonas Mapes.

Mapes's move to Water Street also could have been because he and Elizabeth were preparing for a family. They would have four children, two sons and two daughters. Charles was born in 1800, as was Catherine Deliverance Adeline. They might have been twins, although since Adeline (as she was called) was born at the end of October, she could have been a second child. The name Adeline came from the Mapes family, and Deliverance was Jonas's mother's name. A second son was born in 1806 and named James Jay Mapes after Jonas's father. One family source (Lester D. and Clarence E. Mapes, *The Mapes Family*, 1895) lists the fourth child, also named Catherine, born after James, who married Charles L. Rhodes. James Riker's *History of Harlem*, which is usually reliable, says, "Victor B. Waldron, born February 8, 1798, married Catherine Deliverance Adeline Mapes, October 15, 1822, and had four children. He died on March 3, 1848."[21] In city directories after Waldron's death she is listed as Adeline Waldron, and on her gravestone in Green Wood Cemetery is the following: "C. Adeline Mapes, wife of Victor B. Waldron born October 27th, 1800, and died November 25th, 1878."

Near the turn of the century Jonas Mapes acquired a summer home on farmland in Maspeth, Queens, near the head of Newtown Creek. It was a small colony consisting mostly of farmers, as well as DeWitt Clinton, a nephew of Governor George Clinton, and Judge Garrit Furman, a co-owner of the farmer's market, an anecdotal writer of history, and the squire of a large estate. Both became friendly with Mapes and the three were said to have "chatted, argued, and projected ideas concerning schools for New York City and a canal called Erie, to cross the upper state and connect its two great waterways."[22] These "best friends" would have much to do with each other in the decades to come. Maspeth could be easily reached from Lower Manhattan by sailboat in the warmer months by going up the East River to the entrance of Newtown Creek and thence up to its headwaters. It was an old community, with its first settlers going back to Dutch times. In the 1800s there were several farms linked by good roads to Williamsburg, Jamaica, and Flushing, all on Long Island. Clinton's daughter Mary was born there in 1809, as was Mapes's son James in 1806. James would marry Furman's daughter Sophia in 1827 in the Presbyterian Church in neighboring Newtown.

While Elizabeth Mapes was busy caring for three young children, Jonas was expanding his merchant tailor business and being promoted in the state militia. In 1804 he became a major in the Fifth Regiment, and on April 6, 1807, he was promoted to lieutenant colonel. This promotion was rapidly followed by the order of Daniel D. Tompkins, governor of New York, giving him command of the regiment. He was 40 years old that year and well prepared for the events to come. In November President Jefferson had ordered Governor Tompkins to raise and equip 14,000 militiamen to enforce the Embargo Act of 1807. This was New York's part of a 100,000-man national quota for active service. Mapes's Fifth Regiment was a part of this call up.

CHAPTER SIX

New York City

1800–8

During the 1790s, New York City's population continued to soar, passing its rival Philadelphia, the nation's temporary capital, to become the largest city in the country. This growth continued in the following decade, so that by 1810 the census showed that there were 96,370 New Yorkers compared to 33,131 in 1790, an almost 200 percent increase in 20 years. Immigration from Ireland was largely responsible for this extraordinary increase.

In reaction, the state legislature in 1803 added two new political wards to the city's existing seven, adjusting the boundaries to make the nine wards roughly equal in population. Each ward continued to elect an alderman and an assistant so that the Common Council became a body of 18, with the appointed mayor making the 19th. In the following year the legislature greatly increased the franchise by allowing renters of twenty-five dollars to vote for the first time and by introducing the secret ballot into municipal elections, which in that year was won by the Democratic-Republicans in the Common Council. Many of the new voters were Irish immigrants who supported that party. These changes had come about as a result of the elections of 1800, a watershed in American history.

For the first time the Federalists, who had been in control of the federal government since its founding, lost that control to the Democratic-Republicans. Thomas Jefferson, in his second attempt, was elected president and Aaron Burr was elected vice president. Perhaps the most bitterly fought and one of the closest elections was finally decided by the House of Representatives. In the electoral college the Democratic-Republicans had gained 73 votes to the Federalists' 65 and its candidate, President John Adams. However both Jefferson and Burr received 73 votes, forcing the House to decide who would be president and vice president. After six days and 35 ballots, a congressman from Delaware broke the deadlock, changing his vote to Jefferson. Aaron Burr from New York thus became vice president.

This result was made possible only because in the spring of 1800 all 13 of New York City's seats in the state assembly went to the Democratic-Republicans, giving that party a narrow majority in the Legislature that would choose the federal electors for the fall election. New York State with its large block of electoral votes and Aaron Burr were seen to be responsible for the national party's victory that year.

With George Clinton still in the governor's seat in Albany, with his party in control of the Legislature, and with the New York City Common Council in Democratic-Republican hands for the first time, the Federalists began their long decline as a party in the political life of the country.

The new leaders in power were, of course, President Jefferson in Washington, the new capital; and in New York State George Clinton, his young nephew DeWitt Clinton, and Aaron Burr, the vice president from 1800 to 1804. Edward Livingston became the appointed mayor of New York City. The alliance between Clinton and Burr, both of the same party, was never harmonious and only short-lived. By 1804 Burr had destroyed himself politically by his rash challenge of Alexander Hamilton and the subsequent duel that ended Hamilton's life.

Before disappearing into oblivion after the duel, Burr left one important legacy to his city. In the late 1790s he had taken over control of the Tammany Society from William Mooney and James Tylee and involved it increasingly in local politics with a strong "republican bias." This meant supporting Irish immigrants, dropping its original anti-Catholic stance, and using its growing membership to campaign for Democratic-Republican candidates for local office. It was Burr who set the tone for what Tammany Hall would become in the nineteenth century.

The newcomer among Democratic-Republicans in the landmark elections of 1800 was the governor's nephew. Of Anglo-Irish heritage, DeWitt Clinton was born in 1769 in Little Britain, on the west side of the Hudson

River Valley 50 miles north of New York City. He was the son of Mary De-Witt and the Revolutionary War general James Clinton, a brother of the governor. The young Clinton graduated from Columbia College in 1786, studied law under a leading New York lawyer, and then served as his uncle's private secretary for a five-year term. In 1796 he married Maria Franklin, the daughter of a wealthy New York merchant who left her a sizable inheritance, and immediately entered political life.

With the help of his uncle George, the governor, and his own inborn talent, DeWitt experienced a meteoric rise, starting in 1797 by winning a seat in the state assembly. The following year he moved over to the state senate, and in the Democratic-Republican sweep of 1800 he was elected to the important council of appointment. By gaining control of state patronage he was able to get his colleague Edward Livingston appointed mayor and to solidify his power with many other appointments to city and county jobs. He became known as "the father of the spoils system" in New York.[23]

This was only the beginning. When Livingston was forced to resign as mayor after financial irregularities in the U.S. attorney general's office were uncovered in the city, DeWitt himself was appointed mayor in 1803, after serving for one year only in the United States Senate, thus beginning a long tour of duty that lasted through the War of 1812 until 1815. This ten-year run as mayor was only broken twice (in 1807 and 1810). While mayor in 1812 he ran for president on the Federalist ticket and lost to James Madison, a Democratic-Republican, in his election for a second term. The 1812 election and DeWitt Clinton's later career will be addressed in following chapters.

Several new public buildings appeared in this period, the most important being a new City Hall. Although Federal Hall on Wall Street was renovated only a decade earlier and was still adequate, the Common Council felt that a public "ornament" was needed due to the city's wealth and its future prospects. Such an ornament should be of suitable size and opulence. It also should be located nearer the post-1800 center of activity—further north than on Wall Street. The Council chose the Common or Park as the new site, a triangle between Broadway on the west and Chatham Street (later Park Row) on the east. In a competition for designing City Hall, 26 architects and builders submitted plans. Chosen were Joseph Mangin and John McComb Jr., an architect and a master builder respectively. They designed the exterior together, but soon thereafter Mangin withdrew, nervous about all the changes the Com-

CITY HALL

Aquatint in colors engraved by I. Hill after a drawing by William G. Wall, 1826.
City Hall was designed by Joseph F. Mangin and John McComb Jr. and built from 1803 to 1812
at a cost of $538,000. Mapes was an alderman and member of the Common Council,
from 1813 to 1817, which met in this building.

THE *CLERMONT* ON THE HUDSON

A view of West-Point on the Hudson River with the steamboat invented by M. Fulton going up
from New York to Albany. She made her first trip in 1807, revolutionizing travel over water.
Lithograph by Charles-Balthazar-Julien Févret de Saint-Mémin.

mon Council was demanding. As a result, by the time plans were approved and construction began in 1803, McComb was the supervising architect, who stayed on until its completion in 1811 and got credit for the classical building that exists today.

North of City Hall in what was then called Bowery Village, on the grounds of Dutch governor Peter Stuyvesant's "bouwerie" or garden, a new Episcopal church was completed in 1799. It was named St. Mark's in the Bowery and is still today an active congregation. Located at East 10th Street, it was then way up in the country but was said to have a summertime congregation of two hundred worshipers by 1808.

The city's first public school opened in rented quarters in the Fourth Ward in 1806. It was organized by the New York Free School Society, headed by a wealthy Quaker, Thomas Eddy, with the help of New Yorkers John Pintard, Cadwallader Colden, DeWitt Clinton, and the Free-Masons Society. In Pintard's opinion its purpose was, among other things, to develop "habits of cleanliness, subordination and order in the children of the lower classes."[24] At that time there were private schools available for the privileged.

Periodic plagues continued in New York during the first decade of the new century, forcing the affluent to their country homes that were being built north along the East River and along Bloomingdale Road, the westernmost of two roads to the north tip of Manhattan. In 1803 yellow fever struck again, killing 600 people, followed by another epidemic in 1805. And as the population and congestion grew without any adequate sanitation, cholera became a greater threat.

The year 1807 marked a significant moment in the history of New York City because of two events, one giving great hope to its long-term future, and the other causing a serious, albeit short-term, decline in its fortunes and leading to a serious threat of invasion by Great Britain in 1814. The first event was the successful voyage on August 17, 1807, of Robert Fulton's steamboat *North River Boat* from the Christopher Street dock on the Hudson River upriver to Clermont, home of Chancellor Robert R. Livingston, where it arrived by mid morning the following day, averaging a speed of four and a half miles per hour. Livingston came on board at that time and with Fulton, his partner in the venture, proceeded to Albany, arriving the next day.

Fulton, a Pennsylvania-born Irish-American, had spent years in England and France studying civil engineering. In Paris he met Livingston and the partnership developed. Livingston, with ample funds, was attracted to Fulton's concepts for a steamboat. After building the prototype in Paris, which was successful in trials on the Seine, they decided to return to New York, where Livingston obtained the exclusive rights to operate a steamboat in all of New York's waters.

The *North River Boat*—later renamed the *Clermont*—was built to Fulton's design at Browne's yard in Manhattan in 1806–7. It was 146 feet long, 12 feet wide, flat-bottomed, with an ironwork paddle wheel and a copper boiler. Fulton obtained a 24-horsepower engine from England designed to his specifications. It was all completed for test runs that summer.

After the maiden voyage to Albany, regular service was scheduled from the Cortlandt Street dock. The steamboat was made more comfortable for passengers by providing sleeping cabins, a bar, and restaurant. It quickly became the "fashionable way" to get to Albany and back. By the end of 1812, Fulton had six steamboats in his fleet on the Albany run, and in 1814 he launched the first steam ferry from Beekman's Slip across the East River to Brooklyn. Fulton and Livingston's monopoly of New York waters was extremely profitable for both men, proving that transport by water should be expanded in the future. In 1807 planning began to create a new waterway from Albany west to Lake Erie that, when finished, would insure the future of New York City as the largest port city in the country for years to come.

The second event of 1807 was the signing of the Embargo Act by President Jefferson in late December, which placed a total embargo on all vessels leaving U.S. ports to protect American seamen from being impressed onto British and French ships. The president and Congress had become increasingly angry at the Royal Navy's practice of challenging and boarding American merchant ships looking for British seamen who had jumped ship while in American ports and then shipped out on U.S. merchant ships, where wages were higher. Earlier that year a British frigate had fired on a U.S. merchant vessel, killing an American seaman. Jefferson had then directed British ships to leave American waters, which they ignored. The Embargo Act was the result.

The Embargo Act turned out to be a colossal blunder. It did not hurt British worldwide trade to any great extent, but caused a decade of prosperity in American cities — particularly New York — to come to an abrupt halt. In

1808 exports fell 80 percent, and imports fell 60 percent. Thirty thousand of the forty thousand sailors in the country were laid off. In New York City 120 firms went out of business, 1,200 debtors went to prison, and unemployment skyrocketed. The city entered its first serious depression.

Sailors suffered the most, with 500 ships tied up idle in New York Harbor. Merchants and tradesmen who relied on imported goods, such as tailors who had to import cloth in order to sell apparel, had to close down. As conditions deteriorated throughout 1808 and into 1809, Jefferson held fast to the complete embargo. He did not run for office in November 1808 (Madison was elected then) and would leave office on March 4, 1809. On March 1, the Congress in revolt killed the Embargo Act and adapted a new act that permitted trade with all nations except Britain and France. If either of these two accepted the rights of neutral nations, trade with them could also resume. Jefferson reluctantly signed the bill before Madison took the oath of office. After a 19-month nightmare, conditions in New York slowly improved in 1809, but anxiety continued because relations with Great Britain remained very strained. There was a feeling that conflict lay ahead and that President Madison would not protect the rights of neutral ships any better than had his predecessor.

The political ramifications of the 1807 Embargo Act on New York City gave a huge boost to the fortunes of the fading Federalist Party. Presidents Jefferson and Madison, Democratic-Republicans, took the blame for the economic collapse of the city. Nevertheless, Madison was elected in 1808 against a Federalist presidential ticket of Charles Pinckney of South Carolina and Rufus King of New York. However, in 1809 in New York the Federalists captured control of the Common Council, the state legislature, and the Council of Appointments, as well as the city's congressional representatives. Governor Daniel Tompkins and Mayor DeWitt Clinton remained in office.

CHAPTER SEVEN

Jonas Mapes: His Middle Years

1808–12

From the time Mapes had established himself as a merchant tailor in 1794, his business had prospered as New York City had grown without any interruption both in population and in business activity. As long as ships could come and go freely, the exporting and importing trade would expand, taking advantage of the city's almost unique harbor. Some of the city's merchants, particularly those in shipping and its allied services, were making fortunes like John Jacob Astor, and all were generally experiencing a rise in lifestyle. The population of the city in 1808 was about 90,000, with about 4,000 more in Brooklyn.

In his fortieth year Jonas Mapes could have felt proud. He had risen to the rank of lieutenant colonel in his regiment of the city and county militia. He had become a leader among the city's merchants, and because of the prominence of James Tylee, his father-in-law, he most likely had made the acquaintance of New York's leaders, including Mayor DeWitt Clinton and other members of the Common Council.

His family was complete by that time, with two sons and two daughters who seemed to be healthy. If he thought much about his youth on Long Island, it must have seemed a very long time ago when he left his mother in Stony Brook to "seek his fortune" in New York. The twenty years had passed quickly. His mother, Deliverance, was 64 years old, in good health, and would likely live to the same great age as her own parents did.

Jonas and Elizabeth's lives in New York were undoubtedly brightened by the arrival in the city of Jonas's talented first cousin, Micah Hawkins, the son of Major Jonas Hawkins, his mother's younger brother. Micah had become a successful businessman in the city as well as an accomplished musical performer, a composer, and a painter. About nine years younger than Jonas, Micah had followed the established pattern of apprenticing himself to a tradesman at a very young age — in his case to a coach maker in Morristown, New Jersey, at age 14 — and then moving to Manhattan at 21. Two years later he married the daughter of a Morristown family after starting a grocery business on Catherine Street near the east side docks, not far from Jonas's tailor shop on Water Street.

It was said that Micah "purchased a piano which he played for customers that were shopping, that he was a pleasant conversationalist, possessed a ready vein of humor and was a good singer. He also played the violin and flute in addition to composing songs that were popular and were published."[25] His reputation in the world of entertainment grew from this start. Micah was later credited with composing and writing the first original American opera, *The Saw Mill,* or *A Yankee Trick,* which had a successful run at the Chatham Theater in 1824. Micah died the following year and was buried at Trinity Church, Wall Street. He and his wife had no children.

In 1806 Elizabeth Mapes was listed in the New York Directory as a tailoress living at 35 Lombard Street. This was likely the family home by then, north of Peck's Slip where Jonas had his business. She must have taken in sewing to help the family finances.

With the signing of the Embargo Act in late December 1807 everything would change for the Mapes family and for all New Yorkers. The good times were over. For tradesmen such as tailors, the next two years were marked by unemployment, confrontations, and strikes. In some trades the journeymen formed groups called societies to protect their interests — an early form of union. In 1810 New York experienced its first labor dispute that involved serious violence when journeymen house carpenters converged on Mechanic's Hall and smashed all the windows. Violence against African Americans became common as well.

It should be noted that before the Embargo Act the tailors and shoemakers such as Mapes and Tylee had reorganized the way their businesses were conducted to improve profits and to capitalize their crafts to some extent. It was a transition from the family business to something akin to later methods of mass production. Under this system cloth would be purchased wholesale in large quantities and shipped to New York, usually from England. It was then divided by the merchant and resold to many journeymen tailors, some of whom were masters and some immigrants, who would cut up and sew the final product. The finer quality items would be sold at much higher prices than the lower quality items that were shipped to the south or the west. The merchant could control his costs better, more work was done at the journeymen's homes or in a basement, and less space was required in the merchant's shop. Thus with less space needed and less risk, the merchant tailor could earn a greater profit.

It was probably a combination of this reorganization of the tailoring process and the lack of cloth from abroad during the years of the Embargo Act that forced Mapes to move again. During 1808, the year of deep depression, he moved his shop across the street to 230 Water Street, in the same block but closer to Beekman Street. In 1802 Beekman Street had been opened from Pearl Street east to Water Street. Many old buildings had been torn down, lessening congestion in this crowded neighborhood. To move such a short distance must have meant that he no longer needed nor could afford as large a space. He would remain at this address until 1817.*

After the Embargo Act was repealed in 1809, conditions improved for a few years. The British were much more concerned about Napoleon than about their former colony. During this time the War Hawks in the American congress, led by Speaker of the House Henry Clay from Kentucky and John Calhoun from South Carolina representing Western and Southern interests, pressured Madison to be more aggressive with Britain regarding Canada and with Spain involving Florida. They felt that with a show of military strength the Europeans would give up their colonies. In February of 1812 President Madison and Congress were pushed by the War Hawks to restore non-importation of British goods for a ninety-day period. Finally, on June 18,

---

* The location of Jonas Mapes's tailor shops from 1794 to 1817 at 335 Pearl Street, then 245 and 230 Water Street is today a block or two north of South Street Seaport. That area extends from Beekman Street on the south to Dover Street on the north almost under the Brooklyn Bridge as it enters Manhattan. These are short blocks. One can easily see 230 Water Street from 335 Pearl Street not far away. Pace University lies to the west. On the east side of Water Street are nineteenth-century brick buildings and on the west side is a vacant lot used for parking.

Congress reluctantly declared war. In the House of Representatives the reso-
lution barely passed, with support from the South and West but opposition
from almost all representatives from New England, New York, and Delaware, the principal maritime states. In New York City, led by Mayor DeWitt
Clinton, opposition was very strong. A fear that a return to the depression of
1808–9 would occur and that the city's defenses were entirely inadequate to
stop a British invasion such as occurred in 1776 frightened New Yorkers.
Fifty-six of its principal merchants filed a formal protest with President
Madison. Their fears were soon realized when British frigates set up a blockade off the Narrows entrance of the New York Harbor. The city was sealed off
at the south end.

These events caused a revival in the fortunes of the Federalist Party
both in New England and in New York State. Although a Democratic-
Republican until that time, DeWitt Clinton, as mayor of the largest city in
the nation, became the leader of the opposition to the war against President Madison and was supported by the dominant Federalist Party. He also
had the financial support of almost all the wealthiest merchants in the
Northeast. Old-line Federalists like Rufus King and John Jay supported
him as well, encouraging him to oppose Madison in the presidential election in November 1812. It was the closest election since 1800, but Clinton
lost by failing to win the state of Pennsylvania. He carried all of New England except Vermont, New York, New Jersey, and Maryland. He only won
in his own state, New York, by a slim margin however, as many upstate voters supported Madison, as did the growing number of working class voters
in New York City led by the "new" Tammany Hall and Irish immigrants
who would always vote against Great Britain. From then on Tammany
would oppose DeWitt Clinton's political aspirations. As the war progressed
the New York merchants dropped their opposition and in fact began to finance the national government as a patriotic measure. They were led by
John Jacob Astor, who by 1812 was the most prominent and wealthiest
merchant in the country, with many ships in the prosperous China trade.[*]

---

[*] In 1814 the Democratic-Republican party of Jefferson, Madison, and Monroe changed its name
to the Democratic party.

CHAPTER EIGHT

The War of 1812

1812–15

On June 18, 1812, when war against Britain was declared, Lieutenant Colonel Jonas Mapes was in command of the 142nd Regiment, one of two regiments of infantry in the uniformed corps of the city and county militia of New York. The 142nd was a part of the Third Brigade commanded by Brigadier General Peter Van Zandt and in the First Division under Major General Nathaniel Coles. The Fifth Regiment, which Mapes had commanded after he had received his promotion in 1808, had been reassigned to the Third Brigade and renumbered the 142nd before the war was declared. At that time (April 1812) New York City historian I. N. Phelps Stokes said that "the uniformed corps of the militia of the city and county of New York… consisted of ten regiments of infantry . . . one battalion of riflemen, one squadron of cavalry, three regiments of artillery, one company of flying artillery, one company of veteran artillery volunteers comprising in all about 3,000 men."[26]

Mapes's 142nd Regiment was not ordered to duty, however, until October 1, 1812, when it was placed in service of the United States and ordered to New Utrecht in lower Brooklyn to guard against a possible invasion in the same area where the redcoats came ashore in 1776 at the start of the Battle of Long Island. Mapes's regiment comprised only 600 officers and men and could only warn headquarters if they saw a British fleet approaching. After three months time, with the advent of winter, they returned to New York City and to state control.

The first months of the war saw the British capture the United States fort in Detroit, Michigan. An attempt to invade Canada along the Niagara River by Major General Stephen Van Rensselaer failed for lack of militia support, as did an attempt to capture Montreal by Major General Henry Dearborn. Little preparation for the defense of New York City was made, as it was felt that the four forts protecting the Upper Bay — one at the Battery, two on Governors Island, and Fort Gansevoort on the Hudson River side of Manhattan — together with small forts on Bedloe's, Ellis, and Staten Islands, were sufficient to prevent the entering and landing of a British fleet. The government contract to supply these forts in 1814 was given to Cornelius Vanderbilt, ferryman from Staten Island.

Only at sea in 1812 were there any successes against English forces. In the Atlantic Ocean off Nova Scotia, 700 miles east of Boston, the U.S. Navy's 44-gun frigate *Constitution*, familiarly known as "Old Ironsides," with Captain Isaac Hull in command, encountered the Royal Navy's 38-gun frigate *Guerriere* on August 19, which she defeated after a hard-fought battle. This was a tremendous victory against a Royal Navy warship and a great morale boost to those who thought Britain would not press the war in the west while it was occupied fighting Napoleon in Europe. Captain Isaac Hull had become the first hero of the war.

The British navy did, however, institute a blockade of the entrance to New York by way of the Narrows, sealing off trade for most merchant vessels and causing great economic hardship in the city. Long Island Sound remained open and armed merchant vessels sailed out to prey on British commerce. It was reported that in the first year of the war 125 privateers out of New York brought back 700 prizes captured at sea. The partial blockage lasted until the end of 1813, when the Royal Navy extended it to Long Island Sound and the entire New England coast. Enemy ships were seen in Gardiners Bay sealing off the Long Island ports of Sag Harbor and Greenport.

The threat to New York City from the Royal Navy came not only from its principal bases in Bermuda and Halifax, Nova Scotia, but also from ships in Montreal and in both Lake Ontario and Lake Erie. In 1813 there were several battles on the northwestern front. A U.S. force raided and burned York (now Toronto) and the British captured Fort Niagara and burned Buffalo. It was again a sea battle, which cheered New Yorkers when on September 10 the American navy under the command of 27-year-old Commodore Oliver Hazard Perry defeated a stronger British force in the Battle of Lake Erie, ending the threat from the Great Lakes to New York. Commodore Perry became New York's second hero.

Commodore Perry and Captain Hull were both honored at a dinner given by the grateful City of New York at Tammany Hall on January 11, 1814. Colonel Mapes was chosen by the Common Council to toast Captain Hull. "To Captain Isaac Hull, who opened the door that leads into the temple of our naval glory."[27] They were America's only heroes in the war at that time, and honoring them seemed to help the city's morale in that difficult winter.

By the end of 1813 Federalist opposition to the war had largely disappeared in New York in spite of the economic disaster caused by the complete blockade that made the winter of 1813–14 one of the worst the city had ever known. Patriotism had triumphed. All were ready to protect their city from another invasion of redcoats. Governor Daniel Tompkins and Mayor DeWitt Clinton were ready to lead the defense of the city.

In the annual election of members of New York's Common Council held in November 1813, a new member was chosen by the voters of the Second Ward to be alderman. He was the Federalist candidate, Lieutenant Colonel Jonas Mapes of the city militia. At that time the Second Ward was bounded by Nassau Street on the west to the East River and by Pine Street on the south to Peck's Slip on the north. In the 1810 census there were 7,086 voters in the Second Ward, the second smallest of ten wards.* It was an area where Mapes had had his tailor shop since he came to New York 25 years earlier. Well known and well liked by his neighbors, he was a natural candidate during the war because of his military training and his rank. Also elected as an alderman that year from the Ninth Ward was General Nicholas Fish. In 1814 from the Second Ward Jacob Lorillard, tanning and leather merchant (and later tobacco magnate), was elected an assistant alderman. These two well-known New York names served their city alongside Jonas Mapes.

The Common Council met weekly. Members were assigned to committees that covered all parts of city life, the most crucial of which at that time

---

* In 1813 and 1814 there were ten wards, each electing an alderman and an assistant alderman who were presided over by the mayor and a recorder, making a Common Council of twenty-two.

was the Committee Defense. Mapes served on that committee as well as the Committees for Charity, Ferry, Finance, and Watch in his first year. He was successful in combining his work as an alderman with his military duty as regimental commanding officer. The latter would be particularly demanding in the year to follow.

THE YEAR 1814

During the bleak winter of 1814 the arrival of the frigate *President* in the Upper Bay on February 18 was a surprise that brought some cheer and hope to the beleaguered city. In command was Commodore John Rodgers. Together with *Constitution* and *United States*, *President* was a 44-gun frigate, somewhat lighter but faster than British frigates. The three were the largest ships in the U.S. Navy, known as super cruisers, but they were dwarfed by the Royal Navy's huge 74-gun ships of the line, of which the Americans had none. The task of U.S. captains was to engage and destroy or capture if possible as many British frigates as they could find, while avoiding the huge 74-gun warships. Nelson's *Victory* had been one of the latter.

That February Commodore Rodgers had been returning from a 75-day cruise searching for British frigates and merchant ships to capture. He was within sight of the New Jersey shoreline when *President* encountered a 74-gun British ship of the line bearing down upon her. The strange encounter was described in the following extract from a letter, dated February 22, 1814, from an officer of the *President* to his friend in Providence:

> Situations in which we have been placed this cruise will, I think, add luster to the well-established character of Commodore Rodgers. After passing the light [Sandy Hook], saw several sail, one large sail to the windward, backed our maintop sail and cleared for action. The strange sail came down within gunshot, hauled her wind on the larboard tack. We continued with our main topsail to the mast three hours, and seeing no probability of the seventy-four gunship's bearing down to engage the *President*, gave her a shot windward and hoisted our colors, when she bore up for us reluctantly; when within half a gunshot, backed his maintopsail. At this moment all hands were called to muster aft, and the Commodore said a few but impressive

words, though it was unnecessary, for what other stimulant could true Americans want than fighting gloriously in sight of their native shore, where hundreds were assembled to witness the engagement? Wore ship to engage, but at this moment the cutter being discovered off, backed again to take in the pilot, and the British seventy-four (strange as it must appear) making sail to the southward and eastward. Orders were given to haul aboard the fore and main tacks to run in, there being then in sight from our deck a frigate and gun-brig.

The commander of the seventy-four had it in his power for five hours to bring us at any moment to an engagement; our maintopsail to the mast during that time.

Nineteenth-century scholar and historian Rocellus Sheridan Guernsey describes the aftermath:

The circumstances were not understood until some months after. On returning to England Captain Lloyd called for a court of inquiry and excused himself by alleging a mutiny in his ship; on that charge several of the seamen were executed.

The *President* had to wait seven hours and a half for the tide to rise at Sandy Hook before she could sail over the sandbar, which she did about 5:00 P.M. The frigate *Loire*, of thirty-eight guns, and a schooner, besides the *Plantagenet*, composed the blockading squadron at that time.

The policy of the *President* then entering the harbor of New York, under the circumstances, might well be questioned. The Commodore might have continued his cruise or entered an American port that was not blockaded. When once in New York harbor he was effectually "bottled up," and must stay there, virtually out of the service, or at most, only a further means of guarding the entrance at Sandy Hook bar, and to get out must run the blockade at favorable wind and high tide in the face of the enemy who kept watch of her. It will be remembered that she was rated as a 44 gunship. Her actual metal was 54 guns, and her force was about 420 men. This was a great addition to the force at New York. It was usual at that time when our war vessels passed inside Sandy Hook to come to anchor near there. The *Presi-*

U.S. FRIGATE *PRESIDENT*
ENTERING HARBOR OF MARSEILLES

A watercolor drawing by Antoine Roux. This 44-gun frigate entered New York harbor in February 1814 anchoring off the West Battery to remain there for a year, becoming a mobile fort against attack by the British navy. Her presence may have helped prevent the expected invasion in September 1814.

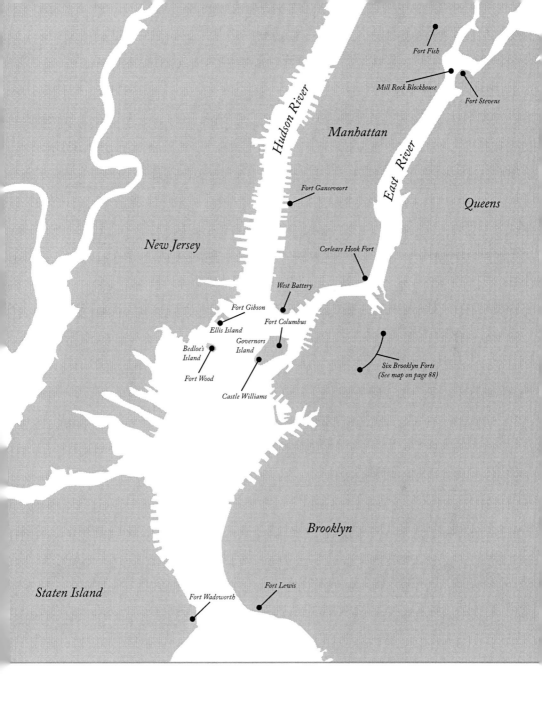

Fort Fish

Mill Rock Blockhouse

Fort Stevens

Manhattan

Hudson River

East River

Queens

Fort Gansevoort

New Jersey

Corlears Hook Fort

West Battery

Fort Gibson

Fort Columbus

Ellis Island

Governors
Island

Bedloe's
Island

Six Brooklyn Forts
(See map on page 88)

Fort Wood

Castle Williams

Brooklyn

Staten Island

Fort Lewis

Fort Wadsworth

FORTS DEFENDING NEW YORK CITY IN 1814

dent anchored near the lighthouse inside the Hook. From that point they were safe from molestation by the enemy, unless there was a concerted attack and siege of New York. A large part of her force could be made available in the harbor defenses and in the land fortifications in case of an attack. She remained there until the next January, as will more fully appear, and her presence may have been enough to have warded off the contemplated attack on New York in the summer of 1814, and to have diverted the enemy to Baltimore and Washington, because they were less protected.[28]

Although for the prior 18 months of the war there had been no active call for the New York City and County militia, a state of readiness was maintained by regular drilling. Some reorganization took place in this interval and some new assignments were made. Notable among these was the promotion of Jonas Mapes, alderman from the Second Ward, to the rank of brigadier general, together with his appointment to command the Third Brigade of Infantry in the First Division. He received this high-ranking promotion on March 2, 1814, and would command the brigade until July 1816, well after the war was over. For that whole time he also served his city as an alderman.

—— ✿ ——

Although not known yet in America, events in Europe in the spring of 1814 would change the strategy of Great Britain in its war against the United States. The long reign of the Emperor Napoleon of France was rapidly coming to its end. By the end of March, Prussian and Russian armies had entered Paris and for much of April discussed with French ministers plans for the restoration of the Bourbon monarchy while the emperor waited at Fontainebleau. On April 20 he fled to Elba off the Italian coast. On May 30, Great Britain and the new French government signed the First Treaty of Paris with terms favorable to the British. Lord Castlereagh's government was thus free to devote more military and naval support to the war in America.

Unannounced, Great Britain began transferring to their bases in Bermuda and in Halifax, Nova Scotia, nine ships of the line, thirteen frigates, and many transports carrying 15,000 Royal Marines and redcoats. This large addition to the force they already had in the Western Hemisphere was intended to end the stalemate that had existed in the sea war. Word of this movement of military might reached America slowly, and not until July were more British warships observed off New York and Long Island. By then an almost complete embargo on U.S. shipping existed in all northeastern coast ports. On July 14 a British force invaded the coast of Maine, seizing the towns of Eastport, Machias, and Bangor before halting at Penobscot Bay. Another raided Saybrook, Connecticut, and on August 9 bombarded Stonington, Connecticut.

Prior to this, on June 15, President Madison had begun to recognize the threat of invasion of New York by naming Major General Morgan Lewis to command the Third Military District, which included the New York area. Rumors were heard of British preparations for invasion from Montreal down Lake Champlain and the Hudson Valley, and of harassing attacks on U.S. ports from their Bermuda base. Their admiral-in-chief Sir Alexander Cochrane, one of Britain's seafaring Cochranes, was known to be in Bermuda, not having moved to Halifax or Montreal.* By July 1 it was quite clear that New York City would be the principal target of a combined attack.

At last, the Common Council of the city was aroused to make plans for more defense, recognizing that the four forts of 1807–12 were inadequate since they were all directed against an invasion through the Narrows from the South. At their meeting on July 6 the Common Council appointed a committee to confer with Governor Tompkins and Major General Lewis about defensive measure to be taken. An open letter to General Lewis outlined three possible avenues for a British assault: one, by vessel from Sandy Hook; two, by troops from Brooklyn, as in 1776; three, by land and sea from Long Island Sound down through Hellgate. The third was the most dangerous, they said, with almost no defenses in place.

The Common Council's Committee of Defense made a full report to the next meeting of the council on July 14. It described in detail the situation in New York City as of that date. It is of particular importance because of the make-up of that committee. Out of its seven members were six aldermen, two of whom, Mapes and Fish, were also generals in the city militia. This group of locally elected officials would take a leading role in the support of their city,

* Sir Alexander Cochrane (1758–1832) was a younger son of Thomas Cochrane, the eighth earl of Dundonald.

together, of course, with Governor Tompkins and Mayor Clinton. They would be greatly assisted by Brigadier General Joseph G. Swift, chief engineer, U.S. Army, a graduate of West Point, who was assigned to the New York Military District by the president and secretary of war. The Committee of Defense report follows:

(Minutes of Common Council July 14th, 1814. The Honorable De-Witt Clinton, Mayor, President)

As directed by the Council, Alderman General Mapes and Thomas R. Smith called on President Madison in Washington D.C. on July 19th. At the meeting was the Secretary of War John Armstrong, a New Yorker. They had a full and attentive hearing and it is but justice to remark that their application received that prompt and early attention which the importance and magnitude of the subject required; and that every disposition was evinced on the part of the Government to comply as far as in their power, with the wishes of this Corporation [the Common Council].

Common Council Minutes July 26, 1814:

As a result of the request the Secretary of War agreed to take the following actions:

To call into immediate service 3,000 militia (the amount requested).

To have the War Department furnish all requisite arms and other military stores as well as ordnance for two fortified Camps — the Troops will also be furnished with subsistence and camp equipage; but their monthly pay is to be advanced by this Corporation [the Common Council] which will again receive it from the General Government.

Proper and skillful officers (General Swift and Colonel Wadsworth [ordnance officer]) will be directed to lay out the proposed camps, to supervise the fortifying the same, and to provide and inspect the ordnance necessary for the purpose.

General Mapes reviewed with Colonel Wadsworth the ordnance that would be provided to New York. The largest pieces included heavy cannon on traveling carriages, eight-inch howitzers, and ten-inch mortars, for a total of 400 pieces, together with needed ammunition. It was agreed that there was an ample store of everything but muskets and that 2000 would be sent from Philadelphia. There was also a difference in the number of militia immediately available. The War Department mentioned 2,600, while the Committee of Defense considered only 1,600. The difference was not resolved.

Mapes and Smith returned to New York after their successful mission and were thanked by the Common Council. Of all the help that was given by the national government to the defense of the city, arguably the most important was that given by Brigadier General Swift, the army's chief engineer. It was his task to design and direct the installations of the defenses for New York City, its harbor, and the surrounding areas of Brooklyn, Long Island, Westchester, and Staten Island. No one knew how much time was available, but all were sure there was not enough for this great task. Everyone's help was needed. This was foremost in the mind of Mayor DeWitt Clinton when he addressed his fellow New Yorkers on August 3, 1814. The address had been approved by the Common Council on August 1.

Clinton began by categorically stating that "in consequence of late events in Europe ... [p]owerful fleets and armies have sailed from Europe!" and challenged New Yorkers to "prepare ourselves for the worst." Saying that it was impossible to determine the place of attack, "it therefore becomes us to be prepared at every exposed point. It is the duty of all good citizens to prepare for the crisis!"

Recognizing that many had been opposed to the war and giving the reasons for such opposition, he asked for that debate to be postponed till a later time. "Now," he said, "we must repulse the enemy from our city in case he attacks us! Shall we refuse to sacrifice our time, our labor, our exertions, our property or even our lives, if necessary, to protect our city, and place it in a state of security?"

He then said that the city has called upon the state and Federal Government for assistance and received from them promises of support, before asking the people of the city to "use all their efforts to cooperate with the government." Recognizing that people had already organized themselves into volunteer work corps, he made four recommendations:

One, to the whole militia of our city to keep themselves in complete readiness to march at a moment's warning and to turn out as frequently as possible for exercise and drill.

Two, to the officers of the militia to closely inspect their men, that everyone may be properly equipped with arms and accoutrements.

Three, to all citizens to offer their services cheerfully to the officers of the United States, to aid by voluntary labor in the completion of the works of defense now being erected and in the construction of others in the months to come.

Fourth, to citizens who have not removed their vessels to do so without delay. "This measure is considered one of great importance. It will take away one of the inducements to a hostile attack. It may prevent the destruction of the city by conflagration, should our shipping be fired by the enemy at our wharves; and it would preserve for our defense multitudes of brave and vigorous men who might otherwise be engaged in removing them in the hour of alarm." Because of the embargo hundreds of ships lay idle at Hudson and East River wharves, a tremendous fire hazard.

Last, Mayor Clinton concluded with challenging rhetoric: "Let there then be but one voice among us. Let every arm be raised to defend our country, and with an humble reliance on the God of our fathers. Our country demands our aid. She expects that every man will be found at his post in the hour of danger, and that every free citizen of New York will do his duty."[29]

The spirited address by the mayor was received with great enthusiasm by the people and produced immediate results. New York seemed to burst with feverish activity. Over the course of the next two months the city made every effort to be better prepared for the expected British attack.

The first step was to receive the plan of General Swift for defense of the city, which the council did on August 8. General Swift's plan took into consideration the fact that the four forts built from 1807 to 1812 were located to defend the city from an attack by ships from the south, and that their guns were supplemented by the 54 cannons on the frigate *President,* still anchored off the West Battery but ready to move where needed. With entry to New York harbor by large warships possible only at high tide, it seemed that an invasion of Manhattan directly from the Atlantic Ocean was the least likely possibility. Since there was no defense at all against an invasion from Long Island Sound through Hell Gate nor any to prevent a landing at a location on Long Island before seizing Brooklyn from the land side as the British had successfully accomplished in 1776, General Swift's plan addressed those two possibilities as his first priority.

NEW YORK FROM GOVERNORS ISLAND

An 1820 aquatint by I. Hill, after W. G. Wall, no. 20 of the Hudson River Portfolio. A part of
Castle Williams is on the right.

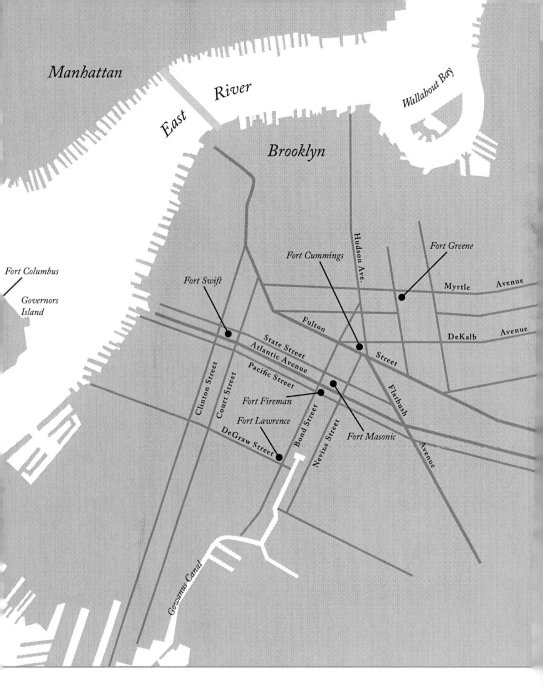

Manhattan

East River

Wallabout Bay

Brooklyn

Fort Columbus

Governors
Island

Fort Swift

Fort Cummings

Hudson Ave.

Fort Greene

Myrtle   Avenue

DeKalb   Avenue

Fulton

State Street

Atlantic Avenue

Street

Clinton Street

Court Street

Pacific Street

Fort Fireman

Fort Lawrence

DeGraw Street

Bond Street

Nevins Street

Flatbush Avenue

Fort Masonic

Gowanus Canal

BROOKLYN FORTS IN 1814

To defend against an overland attack from Coney Island, through lower Brooklyn,
as was made in 1776, six forts were built between Wallabout Bay and Gowanus Creek.
From north to south they were Forts Greene, Cummings, Masonic, Fireman,
Lawrence, and Fort Swift on Cobble Hill.

Forts were needed in Brooklyn, Hellgate, and northern Manhattan. To defend the latter, Fort Clinton (named for Mayor DeWitt Clinton) was built on the eastside of McGowan's Pass, and Fort Fish was on the west side, both to defend against an enemy approaching from the East River. To defend Hellgate, Fort Stevens was built on Hallett's Point in Queens with guns facing toward Manhattan, and a blockhouse was constructed on Mill Rock where the East River and Harlem Creek converge. Both of these could bring heavy fire on ships coming through the dangerous tides of Hellgate.

To defend against an attack by land on Brooklyn, a series of five forts, connected by entrenchments, were built on the high ground south of Wallabout Bay running to Gowanus Creek for a distance of about two miles. As this task was given to General Mapes's Third Brigade, it will be described in more detail. The keystone to the Brooklyn approach was a new fort, Fort Greene, named for the Revolutionary War General Nathanael Greene, which would be located south of the Brooklyn Navy Yard on Wallabout Bay. General Swift's report stated:

> In advance on Brooklyn, Works have been erected which completely insulate it. Fort Greene, (on an eminence overlooking the neighborhood and mounting twenty-three pieces of ordnance, principally of heavy calibers,) and redoubts, Cummings, Masonic, and Fireman, are united by lines of intrenchments resting their right on Gowanus Creek, which runs through a low swampy morass, and having the Wallabout Bay on their left. In each of the redoubts, as well as at the salunt angles of the intrenchments, are planted twelve pounders; the intervals between which do not exceed the half grape shot distance of guns of that capacity. On a small eminence on the east side of Gowanus Creek, is a battery open in the rear calculated for three heavy pieces to defend the mill-dam and bridge, and flanking the right of the lines. To assist, and for the support of this work on the right, stands Fort Lawrence, on a commanding height, within grape shot range. The occupation of which hill became more necessary, as its value would have been incalculable to an enemy succeeding in penetrating the right of the line. In the rear, but within striking distance of redoubts, Fireman, and Masonic, and the adjacent

intrenchments, is the site of Fort Swift; on a conical and imposing eminence [Cobble Hill]. The importance of which becomes enhanced as much as it completely overlooks the strong defences of Governor's Island.[30]

General Swift's plan was submitted to the Common Council of Defense, which included alderman General Mapes, on August 8 and was announced that day in the *National Advocate*:

> Gen. Swift having furnished the Committee of the corporation with a plan for the construction of additional works of defense, near Brooklyn, the work will commence this morning by the artillery company, under the command of Captain Andrew Bremner who have volunteered their services for the day. The committee invite fellow-citizens to follow their laudable example. [...]
>
> To facilitate the business, the Committee of Defence announce that they will meet daily at the Mayor's office in City Hall between the hours of eleven and twelve o'clock to receive tenders of similar services, and to arrange work parties.

Bremner's company was the first group of citizens to volunteer their services for the erection of defenses of New York following the address of Mayor Clinton. All the officers in General Mapes's brigade, consisting of 200 men, were the next.

As August 8 proved to be a very rainy day, Captain Bremner's company was delayed in arriving in Brooklyn until the following morning. However, at 8 A.M. on the ninth they assembled at the site of what would become Fort Greene. They were greeted by General Mapes, who had arrived at an earlier hour. A small ceremony took place, marked by the firing of Bremner's six pounders and attended by Generals Mapes and Swift, after which the building of earth-works began. This event marked the beginning of a huge voluntary effort to protect the city. At the Fort Greene site Captain Bremner's company was followed by groups of tanners and curriers, a society of plumbers, a large force from the Second Ward, and Captain Swain's artillery company of the Third Regiment. The coordination of all groups was carried out by the Committee of Defense of the Council.

General Swift in his report gave credit to the volunteers. "The works . . . have been chiefly constructed by the labor of the Citizens of the City of New York, Long Island, and of the neighboring Towns near the North River, and in New Jersey. All classes volunteering daily working Parties of from Five Hundred to Fifteen hundred Men. The Fortifications are testimonial of Patriotic zeal. Honorable to the Citizens and to the active and assiduous Committee of Defence."[31] According to historians Burrows and Wallace in response to the mayor's call for volunteers "some 23,000 militiamen flocked in from the surrounding countryside. From dawn to dusk they drilled and paraded, and the City Council appropriated money to pay them until they were mustered into regular service."[32]

The construction of the Brooklyn line of five forts with joining redoubts (small forts, protected by artillery) and entrenchments, which was started on August 9, progressed rapidly. On August 15 it was reported that 500 to 1,000 men were at work and that the westernmost fort on Cobble Hill, named Fort Swift after the general, was nearing completion. However work was far from complete on the others when word reached New York by pilot stage on August 17 that 60 ships under Rear Admiral Sir George Cockburn had entered Chesapeake Bay and sailed up the Patuxent River to the west bank village of Benedict, Maryland, where 4,500 Royal Marines under General Robert Ross had landed. His orders were to burn the Capitol, the White House, the Navy Yard, and any other public buildings except the prison — this in retaliation for a similar United States attack on York (now Toronto) in Canada in April 1813. York, with a population of 700 people had been held for 11 days and pillaged before being recaptured by the British.

Prior to the landing in Maryland, Admiral Sir Alexander Cochrane, the British fleet commander, had written to Secretary of State James Monroe that unless America made reparations for the "outrages" in Upper Canada (Ontario), his duty was "to destroy and lay waste such towns and districts upon the [American] coasts as may be found available."[33] This letter was not received by Monroe until after Washington had been burned.

From Benedict it was a 30-mile march across Maryland countryside before reaching Washington. General Ross's marines encountered no opposition until they reached the northwest outskirts at the village of Bladenburg, where they quickly overwhelmed a green militia unit that had been assembled by Secretary of War Armstrong. On the following day they entered a vacated city from which the president and congress had fled and put the buildings to the torch. With their mission accomplished the marines withdrew to their ships on the Patuxent, sparing the town of Alexandria, Virginia, which reportedly had paid General Ross a large ransom for his benevolence.

For the moment New York City had escaped the wrath of the Royal Marines, but it was very concerned about where they would strike next.

Following the raid on Washington, New York took several steps to speed up and buttress its various defenses. On August 27 Governor Tompkins asked Major General Lewis for his plan of operations to defend the city should an attack come by way of Brooklyn or Long Island Sound. Two days later an additional 20,000 militia were called to duty and ordered into national service under General Orders of August 29 by Major General Stevens, First Division Commander. These militia were divided among the Brigades of Generals Morton, Studdiford, and Mapes. All banks in New York and Philadelphia suspended their payments in specie.

The call-up of so many militias presented a serious problem for General Mapes and other brigade commanders: too many officers and not enough privates. At that time General Mapes's Third Brigade consisted of six regiments: the 10th, 51st, 82nd, 125th, 142nd (Mapes's former regiment) and 146th, all from New York City, except the 146th from Staten Island. On September 1 he issued an order to consolidate the regiments to more effectively defend the area of Brooklyn for which he was responsible. This consolidation resulted in many officers not being assigned to duty and led to much dissatisfaction among them. Mapes issued a formal apology on September 4, 1814, thanking them for their service, and hoping that an arrangement might soon be made to give them command.

Among other preparations were those of Governor Tompkins and the Common Council to coordinate a means of notifying all the people of New York should there be a sighting of enemy vessels off the coast either from the south or the east. As Staten Island was one of those important points, it needed to be properly defended. Therefore on September 8 the governor wrote to General Mapes:

> Sir: You are requested to call into service on Monday or Tuesday next week that part of your brigade which is on Staten Island. There are

quarters and tents at the State Works at the Narrows, for nearly seven hundred and fifty men in addition to the force now stationed there. There also are quarters at the Quarantine, and in two public stores, which Mr. Gelston consents should be occupied for four hundred or five hundred men.

I presume, therefore, General Lewis, upon application to him, will order the Staten Island Battalion to encamp in tents at the Narrows, or remove those tents to Red Bank in Princess Bay, and encamp them there or send them to the public buildings at the Quarantine ground; and I must refer you to Major-General Lewis for the purpose. If they are to occupy Quarantine ground, the quarter-master must have some repairs and cleaning done before their arrival.[34]

This letter shows the complications that arose when the state militia was ordered into federal service. Because volunteering for the regular army had slowed to a standstill (fewer than 10,000 men signed up in 1814) and Congress refused to authorize a draft, President Madison was forced to place state militias under federal orders, with regular army officers in charge. New York State accepted this arrangement when it believed it was in peril. Massachusetts, which opposed the war from the beginning, never did. Meanwhile the work at Fort Greene in Brooklyn was nearing completion; Fort Swift, overlooking Governor's Island, was complete; and Fort Lawrence was close to being ready. Fort Greene had 800 feet of barracks, two-thirds with double rooms ready for troops. It would soon be connected with a chain of redoubts and entrenchments to Fort Swift and to Washington Bastion on Jamaica Road (now Fulton Street) near Court Street. Being the largest fort of the chain of five, it became the headquarters of Commodore Stephen Decatur, the country's senior naval officer, who had recently been given command of all naval forces in New York harbor. Four thousand troops had been assigned to Brooklyn by September 15 to properly man the defensive line. They were under the command of General Mapes, ready to defend against the expected invasion from the Atlantic Ocean to the south.

The large cost of this effort to defend the city, to construct the fortifications planned by General Swift, and to pay and equip all of the 20,000 militia called into federal service — all in a very short period — was beyond the means of the federal government in the short run. Therefore the Committee of Defense recommended that the Common Council arrange to borrow $1,000,000 with interest at seven percent from private lenders against the city's credit. This loan, which was quickly fully subscribed, was paid back by the federal government over a period of time. Together with 100,000 days' labor that citizens volunteered to fortify their city, the use of the city's credit was essential to the successful completion of the plan.

By early September 1814 the Committee of Defense not only knew of the disastrous raid on Washington, but it also became aware that a large British force had moved on September 1 south from Montreal to Lake Champlain, crossed the border into New York State, and captured the village of Champlain. It was under the command of Canada's governor general, Sir George Prevost, and consisted of 14,000 men and several supporting British frigates under Captain George Downie that had entered the lake from the St. Lawrence River.* It appeared that the strategy that had failed at the Battle of Saratoga in 1777 was being tried again, a pincer move against New York from the north and an attack from the sea from the south. This time, however, the new nation was much better prepared. It had a respectable navy that had succeeded against the Royal Navy in several sea battles.

On Lake Champlain Commodore Thomas Macdonough had a 14-ship squadron together with 1,500 regulars and 2,500 militia under General Alexander Macomb, a West Point–trained general. Although a much smaller number than Prevost's ground troops, the American ship strength was equal to the British. An American victory on the lake would force the withdrawal of the invasion and end the threat to New York. On September 11 a two-hour naval battle took place in Cumberland Bay near Plattsburg, New York. Commodore Macdonough, with superior tactics and foresight, decisively defeated the British ships, after which Prevost was forced to withdraw to Montreal for lack of support. New Yorkers then knew there would no longer be a threat from the north. But where was Admiral Cochrane's grand fleet?

After sailing out of the Patuxent River into Chesapeake Bay, Cockburn took his battle fleet north past Annapolis before landing about 14 miles south of Baltimore on September 12. This time, however, he encountered a

---

* The British force was part of a 30,000-man army that was sent to Canada, larger than the one sent in the Revolutionary War.

MACDONOUGH'S VICTORY ON LAKE CHAMPLAIN

and defeat of the British Army at Plattsburg by General Macomb, September 11, 1814.
The victory effectively ended the threat to New York City of an invasion from the north.
General Mapes's defense of Brooklyn had yet to be tested.
Line engraving by B. Tanner after H. Reinagle. Published 4 July 1816.

militia who had built a strong line of earth works, and on the march to the city an American sniper killed General Ross. The fleet proceeded to Baltimore Harbor to begin shelling Fort McHenry, its fort at the entrance, but in spite of an all-night bombardment, as the dawn rose on September 14 the Stars and Stripes was still waving, inspiring Francis Scott Key to write "Oh say can you see by the dawn's early light." Fort McHenry was still firing back at the British ships.

Tiring of battle, the admiral called off the attack, reboarded his troops, and sailed south out of the bay into the Atlantic Ocean without attempting any other raid. Most Americans thought the fleet would return to its Bermuda base for ammunition before attempting another attack, and that the next target would be New York City. At that time the total British fleet in North American waters was vast. Under the overall command of Admiral Cochrane were 102 ships of the line, 146 frigates, 96 sloops, 74 brigs, and 58 schooners. Rear Admiral Cockburn was a subadmiral in charge of various task forces of the fleet from time to time.

By the end of September, however, no new attacks had been made, and with the victory by Commodore Macdonough on Lake Champlain ending the threat from the north, New Yorkers were feeling less anxiety. In a letter to Secretary of State James Monroe on September 29, Governor Tompkins said, "For the defence of the City of New York I have exerted myself to the utmost. Full fifteen thousand of the Militia of this State and about One thousand Sea Fencibles, organized under State authority are now in service in the Third Military District. These with Commodore Decatur's command, the regulars, the Sea Fencibles of the United States, Jersey Militia, Corps of exempts and neighboring militias left in reserve, will, if well disciplined and commanded be adequate to the defence of New York."[35]

Despite Governor Tompkins's optimism, the Committee of Defense felt it necessary to urge the militia to keep themselves in a high state of readiness and to finish construction of all the forts in General Swift's plan. In an appeal to the people on October 10, they said, "Having reason to believe that this city is in great danger of attack from the enemy, and that it may reasonably be expected to take place within a few weeks [...] call upon them for a renewal of their patriotic labors without delay for the completion of defences at Harlem."[36] Without these defenses being in full readiness, the approach from the sound through Hellgate was still vulnerable to an attack by sea. In fact, on

October 1 a British frigate was spotted at Pelham Bay scouting out the Hell-gate approach.

Rumors abounded of an invasion by the Royal Navy fleet from Bermuda, only 600 miles away. One of these was that 70 British ships of war were seen off Rockaway Beach heading for Sandy Hook on October 31. Upon investigation it turned out to be false, but seven more ships were anchored in Gardiner's Bay off Eastern Long Island to enforce the blockade, which was already so tight that people on offshore islands were desperate and close to starving. On August 9 Nantucket Island off Cape Cod in Massachusetts actually declared itself neutral and asked for protection and supplies of food from the British.

While the distress caused by the blockade deepened during the fall, peace negotiations in Europe began to make some small progress. On August 8 representatives of Great Britain and the United States had met in Ghent in western Belgium to begin discussions about terms to end the war. With the threat of Napoleon out of the way the British acted as if they had the upper hand by presenting boundary changes between USA and Canada that the former rejected out of hand. These proposals remained on the table for two months without any progress toward an agreement while Washington, Baltimore, and Lake Champlain were attacked and invaded. It was not until after the American victory on the lake and the British failure to capture Baltimore that the British withdrew their boundary proposals, recognizing that America would not accept any at all. From October 31 discussions became more serious. The negotiating team consisted of Treasury Secretary Albert Gallatin; the minister to St. Petersburg; John Quincy Adams; and Henry Clay, leader of the War Hawks and Speaker of the House of Representatives. They quarreled among themselves on several issues, including navigation rights on the Mississippi River and fishing rights on the Grand Banks of Newfoundland. All that could be agreed on was to return to prewar status quo conditions, which also suited the British because the issues of impressment of seamen and search of vessels were not mentioned at all. With the French navy no longer a factor, the British were eager to end the blockade and to resume importing cotton from the American southland. Both sides were weary of war.

A peace treaty was signed on December 24 in Ghent. It provided that all prisoners of war and captured territory were to be returned. All boundary disputes were to be referred to a boundary commission that would be set up by the two countries. Both pledged to end the slave trade. No other issues were mentioned at all. Britain never gave up its search rights but used the practice less frequently. What was significant was that for the first time Great Britain recognized the United States in an official document that accepted the borders of the new country. The groundwork had been laid for a peaceful relationship. Henry Clay summed up the treaty saying "that those latest terms were not unfavorable since America had lost no territory and no honor."[37] His attitude as a War Hawk had greatly changed since 1812.

Although the peace treaty was signed on December 24, word of it did not reach the Western Hemisphere for almost two months, during which time the largest battle of the war was fought.

After Admiral Cochrane left the Chesapeake Bay on September 15, his fleet had returned to Bermuda for resupply, but upon arrival he received new instructions from the admiralty in London. He was to proceed with his army of 5,000 men under General Ross (who they believed was still alive) southward to the Caribbean, to rendezvous at Jamaica with an even larger fleet under way from Europe with an army of veterans of the Duke of Wellington's Peninsular Campaign. When the admiralty learned of Ross's death, the duke's brother-in-law, Lieutenant General Sir Edward Pakenham, was sent out to lead the army in an attack on New Orleans. From the British point of view this new strategy was preferable to an invasion of New York, which was well defended with cannon and would occur at a time when the weather was cold and stormy.

Throughout September and October, New York waited for the invasion that would never come. In spite of warnings that the city was still in great danger, the militia was becoming restless. Units of General Mapes's Third Brigade that were quartered at home were drilled every morning from 6:00–8:00 A.M. and every evening from 4:00–6:00 P.M. at various parade grounds. They also performed guard duty at the Brooklyn forts and redoubts. Militia from upstate and New Jersey who were away from home at harvest time were especially unhappy, and there were some dissension in the ranks. Morale began to deteriorate to the point where some change was needed.

On October 14, President Madison as commander-in-chief relieved Major General Morgan Lewis as commander of the Third Military District and replaced him with Governor Tompkins (with the rank of major general), although he did not hold a commission in the U.S. Army. Tompkins, a younger man, was a popular governor, particularly with the younger militia, and also was a Democrat, which appealed to the upstate militia. He left Albany for New York City on October 27 to take up his new assignment.

Governor Tompkins visited the military forts in Harlem and at Fort Greene in Brooklyn on the following day and then the others protecting the harbor. From November 10 to 15 he reviewed all the militia in the district. General Mapes's Third Brigade was reviewed on November 15 on Stuyvesant Field near Waterbury's ropewalk. Here the governor was joined by Major General Stevens and Generals Studdiford and Mapes and their respective suites. General Mapes's brigade consisted of the regiments of Colonel Dodge, Colonel Van Hook's city regiment, and Colonel J. R. Van Rensselaer's battalion from Columbia County. The latter had the reputation of being the best-drilled and equipped body of militia in the service at that time. It was then 1,800 strong. The reviews were held to keep up the morale for a few more weeks, as no one was any longer expecting an attack.

On November 14, Colonel Solomon Van Rensselaer, the adjutant general, wrote to his wife in Albany: "If there is no attack on this place [New York City] this fall — and none is expected — I shall be with you in a few weeks, when the Governor will return to Albany.*

"The militia are sickly and heartily tired of military life; desertions are frequent and furloughs asked for by the dozens every day. . . . Last night we returned from again visiting the troops on Long Island and the Narrows a tour of three days I spent very pleasantly, in which twice we reviewed three Brigades, and were received at the different posts with a tremendous roar of cannon. . . . We are just now going out to review the troops."[38]

Finally, on November 28, 1814, the governor issued an order to the militia to stand down throughout the New York City area, to return their arms to the state arsenal, and to return home to their families. Colonel Van Rensselaer wrote, "Ten thousand troops were under arms, marched through the city and were reviewed by the Governor, after which we dined in the City Hall by invitation of the Common Council. All idea of an attack by the enemy has been given up."[39] General Mapes was doubly pleased that day, as he had just been reelected for a second year as an alderman from the Second Ward. He had become something of a local celebrity.

---

* Solomon Van Rensselaer was the nephew of Major General Stephen Van Rensselaer.

The only ominous news to reach New York in December that year was that the British navy had captured a small American fleet off Louisiana, giving them command of the route to New Orleans. In spite of all the good feeling in New York, Britain still ruled the sea.

THE BATTLE OF NEW ORLEANS

The British armada that assembled in Jamaica on November 24 was larger than the Spanish Armada that had sailed against them in 1588. Under the overall command of Admiral Sir Alexander Cochrane were 60 ships carrying 10,000 sailors, 1,500 marines, and 11,000 British soldiers, including some of the most celebrated regiments in the army that had won battles when led by Wellington in the Peninsula Campaign. In command of the army was Major General John Keane — temporarily, as General Sir Edward Pakenham was still sailing across the ocean. His absence was significant, as the young, inexperienced Keane acquiesced to the older Cochrane in the critical decision of where and how to attack New Orleans.

Cochrane had known since September that an invasion at New Orleans would place the British army up against the best general that America could offer, General Andrew Jackson. Jackson had been in the southeast fighting Indians and was known for his hatred of anything British "with an implacable fury that was absolutely devoid of fear."[40] He was fiercely independent, particularly of orders from Washington, and evoked great loyalty from his men. In September he had bested the British at Fort Bowyer at the mouth of Mobile Bay and again in November had driven them out of Pensacola, Florida. He moved from Mobile to New Orleans on November 22 when it seemed that the British would land there, leaving behind a strong garrison both at Mobile and Pensacola.

With those two ports strongly defended there were only two options for Admiral Cochrane to choose for an always-dangerous amphibious landing to attack New Orleans. One, at Barataria Bay south and west of the city that was in the hands of the unfriendly pirates of Jean Laffite; the other through Lake Borgne south and east of the city. He chose the latter in spite of the fact that the lake was so shallow that all but the smallest ships in the fleet had to anchor outside the lake, with the troops having to be barged for sixty miles across the lake to solid ground. It sounded like a recipe for disaster, but Cochrane was sure that the redcoats would not fail. While in Jamaica he had 40 shallow-draft barges built to get the army across the lake. It was not possible to sail large warships up the Mississippi River because of the unfavorable current and many shoals at that time, to say nothing of two forts along the way.

The British fleet left Jamaica on November 26. They were observed passing Pensacola on December 8 by friendly Indians and on December 12 arrived at the anchorage east of Lake Borgne. It was just as General Jackson had predicted. There was no element of surprise at all. Admiral Cochrane saw that his first task against the Americans was to clear the lake of their gunboats. This only took a couple of hours on December 14, as there were only five of them. The first battle of this campaign was a complete victory for the powerful British fleet.

With Lake Borgne clear, Cochrane began a week-long effort to row the entire army across the lake in two stages: first a 40-mile journey to Pea Island, and then, after some reconnaissance, a 30-mile journey to a point chosen where the army could reassemble and march on the city. No opposition appeared during this entire week, lulling Admiral Cochrane and General Keane into believing that New Orleans could be captured quickly. On the morning of December 23 the local invasion began with Cochrane saying that he would be having his Christmas dinner in New Orleans.

No sooner had the British forces assembled and moved to a point near the Mississippi River late in the evening on December 23 than General Jackson attacked them when most were exhausted from the long boat ride across the lake. He had also ordered the *Carolina* to sail quietly downriver to a point opposite the British camp before opening fire with its cannons at night. The British were caught by surprise, the night battle went on until midnight, when Jackson wisely withdrew, as he was vastly outnumbered. It was first blood and a victory for the Americans. The next two days, Christmas Eve and Christmas morning, General Edward Pakenham arrived with the last of the British Army to relieve General Keane. He was a week later than expected due to a slow voyage from Europe, and he had little time to plan his strategy for the advance north on the city.

The British forces were cheered by Pakenham's arrival. He was an experienced general who had fought under Wellington at Salamanca in Spain, and they were confident that he had learned much from the man considered the finest general in England, if not the world. Pakenham, however, was appalled by the situation in which he found the army, lodged between a river and a swamp with little room to maneuver and with a supply line that depended on small boats that had to be rowed sixty miles across a lake in the middle of winter.

First, he decided to silence the U.S. Frigate *Carolina* with a shore battery on December 27. Second, he planned a frontal assault on the American defensive line before it was finished. This was called a daytime "reconnaissance" and took place on December 28. The line was situated about five miles south of New Orleans on the east bank of the Mississippi at Chalmette Plantation. Pakenham determined that Jackson was still building earthen barricades with redoubts and trenches from the river, across the plain to well into the swamp. It was an excellent defensive fortification that would give cover to his 3,600-man militia while his Kentucky sharpshooters could fire at the enemy. It would be very difficult to break by a frontal assault and impossible to outflank due to the river and swamp. Only along the west bank of the river could Pakenham send troops against little opposition around the line to New Orleans, but he tried that only at the last moment with much too small a force. Meanwhile, as the British withdrew from their "reconnaissance attack," Jackson continued to make his line even stronger.

Ironically, Admiral Cochrane had planned the attack on New Orleans along a route that provided General Jackson with the best defensive site he could have asked for. And General Pakenham arrived too late to change the overall strategy. He planned for a full-scale assault on the line on January 1, and when that failed, for another final effort on January 8. Because of a series of tactical errors, such as not bringing ladders up to the line to mount the barricades, and the failure to move up the west bank in sufficient force to outflank the main line, the general's plan of attack failed. Pakenham himself was killed by rifle fire, as was his assistant general, and British casualties were ten times greater than American. However, the British never formally surrendered. Following the January 8 battle, the general then in charge, John Lambert, decided to withdraw back to the ships across Lake Borgne, which took more than a week to accomplish. Jackson had saved New Orleans, but in his mind he wondered where the British fleet would strike next. Although he did not know it, the fleet had been reinforced by two more regiments that had arrived after the January 8 defeat.

From outside of Lake Borgne, Admiral Cochrane took his huge 60-ship fleet to attack Mobile, Alabama, determined to achieve some victory over the Americans. They besieged Fort Bowyer at the head of Mobile Bay and forced its surrender on February 11. However, before the admiral could organize an attack up the bay on that city, word reached him of the peace treaty that had been signed on December 24. A disappointed man, Admiral Cochrane sailed home to England with his fleet and 10,000 men just in time for action at Waterloo, where Wellington was preparing for his great contest against Napoleon who had returned to France on March 1 from Elba. He would need every man for that gigantic battle to come.

LAST VESTIGES OF THE WAR

Before the arrival of the peace treaty in New York on February 11, 1815, belligerent acts were undertaken by the United States as well as by the British in New Orleans. For almost a year the frigate *President* had laid at anchor off the West Battery protecting New York harbor after having successfully run the British blockade. Her guns never had to be fired, but she stood ready at all times. With the threat to New York over, for the winter at least, Commodore Stephen Decatur was anxious to get to sea again with his flagship. Many British vessels were known to be in American waters, targets for capture with prizes on board. New York was still under a blockade, however, which would have to be passed at night if *President*, *Hornet*, and *Peacock* were to get free undamaged. The British squadron consisted of five ships led by *Endymion*, with 40 guns.

On Saturday evening, January 14, 1815, the wind and tide were favorable. *President* with 425 men aboard weighed anchor and silently departed the safety of Sandy Hook, hoping that by daylight they would be far out to sea and away from the blockading ships. A letter from Commodore Decatur gives a firsthand account of events that followed:

> The night we left the Hook, owing to some blunders of our pilots, we struck on the bar and there remained thumping for two hours until the tide rose. At daylight we fell in with the British squadron, consisting of the *Majestic*, *Endymion*, *Pomona*, *Tenedos*, and *Despatch* brig. My ship, owing to her getting aground, lost her sailing. I lightened

her as much as possible, but the enemy gained on us. The *Endymion*, mounting 24-pounders on her gun deck, was the leading ship of the enemy. She got close under my quarters and was cutting my rigging without my being able to bring a gun to bear upon her. To suffer this was making my capture certain, and that, too, without injury to my enemy. I therefore bore up for the *Endymion* and engaged her for two hours, when we silenced and beat her off. At this time the rest of the ships had got within two miles of us. We made all the sail we could from them, but it was in vain. In three hours the *Pomona* and *Tenedos* were alongside, and the *Majestic* and *Endymion* close to us. All that was now left for me to do was to receive the fire of the nearest ship and surrender; for it was in vain to contend with the whole squadron. My loss has been severe, the precise number I do not know, but I believe it to be between 80 and 90; of this number 25 are killed. Babbitt, Hamilton and Howell are among the slain.[41]

The firing of cannons in this battle was said to be heard in Stonington, Connecticut, and Newport, Rhode Island, which would indicate that it occurred in Rhode Island Sound off the end of Long Island. The American losses were far greater than the British. The *President* as a captured ship was taken to Bermuda, where the prisoners aboard were freed to return to the United States or go elsewhere as they chose, as the peace treaty had been received in Bermuda. Commodore Decatur returned to New York to be assigned a new task in the Mediterranean against Algeria, where he ended the reign of the Barbary pirates. He died in 1820 as a result of a duel with a navy captain.

After its defeat and capture, it was thought that news about the sailing of *President* on the night of January 14 had been given to the British 12 hours before its departure. Consequently a British ship, *Majestic*, which had been laying off Plumb Island (off Orient Point, Long Island) on Sunday morning, went to sea in great haste before sunrise, leaving its water caskets on the island. It intercepted *President* shortly thereafter.

The *Hornet* and the *Peacock* passed the blockade safely and sailed on a cruise to the East Indies. The last sea battle of the war was fought on March 23, 1815 (three months after the peace treaty had been signed), when *Hornet* captured the British ship *Penguin* at the port of Tristan d'Acunha in the South Atlantic Ocean. Word finally reached her after her victory that the war had ended.

News of the Treaty of Ghent was first received in America in New York City on February 11 with the arrival that day of the British war ship *Favorite* under a flag of truce. It had been a very cold winter that year. The Hudson was frozen over across to Jersey City, and the sound was frozen to Sands Point. For many days no vessels arrived at the port due to ice conditions. However, in the afternoon of February 11, *Favorite* met *Endymion* still on blockading duty off Sandy Hook and advised her that she carried special messengers, British and United States envoys, with the peace treaty. She requested permission to approach Sandy Hook under a flag of truce. Once there she was allowed to proceed past the forts and to land in Lower Manhattan. Word from the U.S. envoy aboard *Favorite* first reached the office of the *Gazette* paper in Hanover Square and from there quickly spread throughout New York City. "The cry of Peace! Peace! Peace! was heard everywhere. No one stopped to inquire about free trade or sailor's rights. No one even inquired whether the national honor had been preserved. . . . It was enough that the ruinous war was over. . . . Never was there such joy in the City."[42]

Word reached Washington 30 hours later and spread to other cities: Boston, Philadelphia, Providence, and Albany. The reaction was much the same: America was tired of war. The Senate of the United States quickly confirmed the treaty on February 16, and President Madison signed it the following day.

New York City quickly planned to celebrate the peace on February 22 with a grand array of fireworks in front of the government house, with the firing of guns at the Battery at seven o'clock in the evening and an illumination of all homes in the city. Also it recommended that flags be displayed during that date from the forts and from the vessels in the harbor and that a salute be fired at noon when the bells of the city churches would be rung for an hour. This joyous occasion was not held on February 22 as planned, however, but was postponed until the twenty-seventh. Politics had reared its head. The twenty-second being Washington's birthday and the first president having been a Federalist, the governor and mayor decided to postpone it to accommodate Democratic sentiment against the city's Federalists who they felt were less than wholly loyal during the war. On December 15, 1814, at Hartford, Connecticut, the New England Federalists had debated whether to secede from the Union in their anger over the war. With the arrival of the peace treaty, the crisis passed and no vote was taken.

CHAPTER NINE

Postwar New York

Daniel D. Tompkins

On February 22, 1815, with the war over, Governor Tompkins addressed the militia of the State of New York, expressing "his praise and gratitude for the promptitude and fidelity with which they have on all occasions obeyed those various calls of service in defense of the State, which its safety compelled him to make."[43] He also thanked them on behalf of President Madison for their service to the country.

Tompkins himself had made a major contribution to New York and the nation as a whole. Elected governor in 1807 at the age of 33, he served for ten years. He was called "A Great War Governor" by historian D. S. Alexander.[44] Historian Alexander C. Flick said, "Confronted during most of the war with a hostile Assembly [dominated by anti-war Federalists], hampered by an inadequate staff, an inefficient militia system, and a lack of funds, he devoted his great energy and very considerable ability to the conduct of war, risking both health and fortune for the cause."[45]

The reference to "risking his fortune" refers to his effort in September 1814 to finance the defense of New York City when the credit of the United States was so poor that banks would not underwrite loans for defense unless the governor personally endorsed the notes with his signature, thus guaranteeing them and putting himself at great financial risk. Afterward it was determined that the war cost New York State $1,959,417 in total.

As for "the inefficient militia system" that had existed when the Republicans swept the state in April 1814, Governor Tompkins called for a special session of the legislature in September to consider his proposals to revamp the militia. The measure became law on October 24, too late to help with the war but of benefit to the militia in the future. The most important features of the new law were to provide a two-year service requirement instead of three or six months and to distribute the burden of military service more equitable, according to wealth. It did, however, allow wealthy persons to hire a substitute, which would become a common practice during the Civil War, still 55 years in the future. Generally the militia was strengthened by these changes, and Governor Tompkins was reimbursed by the state for monies he spent for defense. In spite of the governor's efforts, the American militia was looked down upon by the English for years to come.

During 1819–20, Charles H. Wilson, an Englishman, visited America. Among his many disparaging comments about New York was one regarding military personnel, which he made after watching the Fourth of July parade in the city: "The parade next demanded a visit; the commanding officer [General Mapes] I found a tailor. . . . The singularity of a tailor commanding 5,000 men I considered strange, because the old adage with us is, that for the manufacture of one man, nine snippies are requisite. . . . Curiosity led me to enquire if such was usual for officers to be mechanics, or other occupations, and found it was so; Generals, Corporals, Colonels, Fifers, Majors, Drummers, Captains, Privates, Lieutenants, Sergeants, Ensigns, Pioneers and all, when divested of the pride and pomp of glorious war, retire inglorious to ignoble avocations, with 'their blushing honors thick upon them,' and recount their chivalrous deeds, hair-breadth scapes and all the gallantry of the deadly breach, in the saw-pit or the cobbler's stall."[46] No comprehension of a voluntary militia army was shown in these remarks of someone brought up in the English class society where the military stood above and apart from merchants and tradesmen. The lines were seldom crossed.

After leaving the governorship of New York, Tompkins became vice president under President James Monroe from 1817 to 1825. Shortly after leaving that office he died at the age of 51 and was buried in the cemetery of St. Mark's Church in Stuyvesant Square.

DEWITT CLINTON

Having served as mayor of New York since 1803, with the exception of years 1807 and 1810, DeWitt Clinton resigned on March 6, 1815, to begin his efforts to become governor of the state, which were successful in 1817, when he succeeded Tompkins. Clinton's political opponents engineered the appointment of Tammany chief John Ferguson to the mayoralty with the understanding that he would shortly resign to become surveyor of the port, a highly lucrative office. On July 10, Ferguson was replaced by Jacob Radcliff, who had previously served one term.

The Common Council's Committee of Defense did not submit its final report until November 6, 1815. After reviewing all actions taken from the beginning of the war it concluded by saying that these defensive measures likely preserved it from attack and from the fate that befell Washington D.C. Also that had the enemy attacked, they would have been repulsed as they were in New Orleans. They urged that the city's defenses be maintained in readiness for future use if necessary. And in concluding they paid special tribute to Brigadier General Joseph G. Swift, who designed the defense plan, by naming him a benefactor of the City of New York. It was signed by the Committee of Seven, including Jonas Mapes, alderman.

General Mapes was reelected alderman on December 4, 1815, to serve his third consecutive one-year term. During this term, which would be his next to last, he was appointed to the finance committee on January 3, 1816 and on May 6 was elected charter officer for the city. He was also appointed on that date to three standing committees: on defense, ferries, and canal. The latter committee was a new one, having jurisdiction over the city's interest in the Erie Canal, which was in the very early planning stage at that time. The council in February had petitioned the state legislature its strong support of the project and commented that it should be as straight as possible so barges could be drawn by horses; that the minimum number of lakes should be created; and that the part near the Hudson should be built first. This petition on behalf of the whole Common Council was signed by Mapes, Lorillard, and three other members.

Canal commissioners were appointed by the legislature on April 17 that

year. Stephen Van Rensselaer, DeWitt Clinton, Samuel Young, Joseph Elli-
cott, and Myron Holly were directed to have the proposed route explored.
More on the Erie Canal will follow.

July 8, 1816, was a memorable day in the military life of General Mapes,
for on that day, at age 47, he received his second star with promotion to the
rank of major general. The order of Governor Tompkins was signed by Adjutant General Solomon Van Rensselaer assigning General Mapes command of
the First Division of New York State Infantry, which included the 22nd, 33rd,
and 44th Brigades. The promotion, a great honor, was to the highest military
rank that had been achieved in the United States with the exception of George
Washington, who during the Revolutionary War held the rank of lieutenant
general with three stars. And not again was it given until the Civil War in
1864, when General Grant was awarded a third star. After Governor Tompkins retired to become vice president, it was noted in the *New York Evening
Post* on March 31, 1817, that "about 200 officers of General Morton's division
of artillery and Gens. Mapes's and Ward's divisions of infantry held a public
dinner at the City Hotel in honour of Vice-President Tompkins." There was
always a close feeling between the governor and his militia officers, and particularly so with Daniel Tompkins, who during the war was very well liked by
the officer corp.

Although Mapes's military career had been successful by any standard,
his business as a merchant tailor was filled with ups and downs. He was not
listed among merchants with assets greater than $5,000. These ups and downs
coincided with those of the many other tradesmen who depended on the
activity of ships docking along the East River piers. From the time of the
1807 embargo until after the 1812 War was a serious downtime. After 1815
conditions began to improve.

CHAPTER TEN

The City Revival

1815–24

As soon as the ice left the rivers after the hard winter of 1815, an immense quantity of foreign goods entered the port of New York. In the months of April, May, and June the customs house reported receiving $3,900,000 in duties. And during three days in August, 65 vessels entered the harbor laden with goods to sell. Imports increased so quickly that demand could not keep up and the market collapsed. Thus the winter of 1815–16 saw great distress with a short but hard depression throughout the whole country. However good times soon returned and the country and city entered a period of great prosperity that would last for 20 years (1817–37), with the exception of a short downturn in 1819.

The population figures reflected this change. From 1810 to 1816 during the embargoes and the war, New York City's population increased only by 4,200, from 96,370 to 100,570. But from 1816 to 1820 the gain was 23,000, to a population of 124,000. In that year New York State became the most populous in the nation, and the city far outstripped all others in its growth rate. This growth was in large measure due to immigrants from England and Ireland who entered the city and remained there. By 1825, New York City had grown to 162,000, a 62 percent increase in ten years.

Although improvement was expected and did come about in 1815 and 1816, misfortune occurred on the night of December 3, 1816, when "a destructive fire in the neighborhood of Water Street and Beekman Slip (later named Fulton Street) burned about 25 buildings to the ground and severely damaged many others. Nearly 20 fireman were injured by falling timber."[47] With wooden buildings packed closely together it could have been much worse. The city's oldest market, the Fly Market built in 1699, had been closed earlier in the year and was to be replaced by the Fulton Market in 1821. Located between Beekman Slip and Beekman Street, it had also been the site of a slave market. What remained of the market was totally destroyed in the fire.

Mapes's tailor establishment at 230 Water Street was very near the intersection at Beekman Street, and was thus within a short block of the buildings lost in the blaze. It is not known if it was destroyed, but it must have been damaged in such an inferno. In any event, Mapes did move that winter, opening his new tailor shop in 1817 at 31 Wall Street at the corner of William Street.

This location was only a half-mile away from his Water Street shop and two blocks further inland. Wall Street by then had become the street of banking houses, with only a few shops and private houses. However the new site was closer to Broadway, a substantial advantage, as that great thoroughfare was "the most frequent promenade where all new fashions can first be admired. In the cool season and when the weather is fine the young dandies and the fair sex promenade on the sidewalks between two and three in the afternoon."[48] It was also known as the Bond Street (the elegant shopping district in London) of New York, with shops on both sides filled with everything useful and fashionable. Mapes had taken on a partner by that time, and the firm of Mapes and Oakley, merchant tailors, became more in the public eye and easier to reach from Broadway or when a customer was going to his bank on Wall Street.

Mapes's family in 1817 consisted of his wife, Elizabeth, and their four children: Charles and Adeline, both age 17, James, age 11, and Catherine, the youngest. They lived at 58 Broad Street, only a short walk from the tailor's shop. Jonas was looking forward to having Charles join him soon as an apprentice in the family business.

Success had enabled Jonas to have a town house near his friend Judge Garrit Furman in the area of the Battery, a pleasant place where many of New York's leaders were living. He and Elizabeth had a garden there with

BROADWAY FROM THE BOWLING GREEN

Aquatint drawn and engraved by William J. Bennett, 1834. Looking north up Broadway.
Trinity Church spire is on the left side of Broadway. The most fashionable residences were in this area
during General Mapes's lifetime. Number One Broadway, the building on the extreme left, was the
residence of Sir Henry Clinton and Sir William Howe during the Revolutionary War.

ELIZABETH TYLEE MAPES (1777–1868)

At the request of the Common Council, General and Mrs. Mapes sat for portraits by Samuel L. Waldo. He was a Royal Academy–trained portraitist who had settled in New York and painted many prominent men and women.

ELIZABETH, GRANDMA MAPES IN HER OLD AGE

A photograph by K. W. Beniczky

fruit trees described later by their granddaughter, Mary Mapes Dodge, as follows:

> Grandmother lived in a city house, but it had such a big green garden that, when you looked out of the back windows, you felt almost as if you were in the country. There were flowers and shrubs and grape-vines in it, a currant-bush near the pump, and a real live apricot-tree that grew up in one corner straight past the drawing-room window, and nearly up to the windows of grandmother's chamber. When the apricots were ripe, it was fun to jump up and try to catch one, if you were in the garden; or if you were in the drawing-room it was as pleasant to reach out and try to pluck the nearest; or even if you were in grandma's room, and nobody was there to scream that surely you would fall and break your neck, it was grand sport to reach down and try to catch one of the lovely little things with the hooked handle of grandma's green parasol. Not that you could ever get one in any of these ways—no, indeed. The tree seemed enchanted, and held its tender, peachy treasures among its bright leaves as firmly as though they were frosted gold; for, you see, they were always just a quarter of an inch beyond the reach of any one unless he or she were in the tree. Grandma's colored man, Robert, who took care of the horses, sometimes would stand on the pump and reach down a few for us; but the time of times was when grandma allowed us to hold quilts and things under the tree while Robert shook it. Oh! But unless you are very little, and have grandma, and the grandma has such an apricot tree in her garden, and every apricot on it is soaked through with sunlight and sweetness, you can't possibly understand it, after all.[49]

The winter of 1817 turned out to be one of the coldest of the nineteenth century. So much ice formed in the Hudson and East Rivers that ships could not dock at piers and had to wait in the harbor for warmer weather. The *Evening Post* reported on February 4, 1817, "This morning the ice stuck fast in the East River and formed a complete bridge from Brooklyn to Peck-slip [in Manhattan] on which several ladies and hundreds of gentlemen crossed and recrossed without the least difficulty. . . . The North River [Hudson River] also was frozen over".

With the advent of spring, travelers from abroad came to America with increasing frequency, arriving on sailing vessels that took at least a month for the westward passage. One of these, Englishman John Palmer, described the city he visited in 1817.

> Several of us took lodgings at Greenwich [Greenwich Village in Manhattan today], a pleasant and populous suburb of New York. Price of board and lodging, four dollars or eighteen shillings sterling per week. At the best taverns and boarding-houses in the city, you cannot be boarded and lodged under two dollars per day.
>
> The things that most struck me on my first walks in the city were the wooden houses, the smallness, but neatness of the churches, the colored people, the custom of smoking segars [cigars] in the streets (even followed by some of the children), and the number and nuisance of the pigs permitted to be at large; as to the rest, it is much like a large English town.[50]

On April 15, 1817, the New York State Legislature passed three acts. One authorized the commencement of the building of the Erie Canal, which would greatly benefit all New Yorkers. The second incorporated the New York Institution for the Instruction of the Deaf and the Dumb, a great interest of General Mapes, who was one of its first promoters. A school was opened in May 1818 in Washington Heights. It was only the second such school for the deaf and the dumb in the country, the first being in Hartford, Connecticut, started by Thomas Gallaudet the year before. The third act passed a law equalizing the population of the ten wards, which would dramatically change their size and their political make up. A Federalist paper called this an act "to gerrymander the wards in this city." For General Mapes, a Federalist in a dying party, it meant his end as an alderman. When his term was over on May 12 he retired from office, not choosing to run again in such a heavily Democratic ward. He had served his city tirelessly for three and a half years—one in wartime—as part of a body that had been responsible at the most basic level for the city's governance and development.

Although Mapes had resigned as an alderman, he maintained his service and rank in the state militia. In a realignment in 1818 he was assigned command of the Second Division of Infantry, which included the 44th and 45th

Brigades. He also saw with great interest that in June of that year, 20-year-old Victor B. Waldron was commissioned an ensign in the militia. Young Waldron was working in the tailor shop of Mapes and Oakley. It must have brought back memories of his own commissioning 24 years earlier.

Following the war, concern grew about the many who were out of work, whose numbers were increasing with the arrival of immigrants from Ireland. As imported goods also began arriving again, there was not enough purchasing power in the population to absorb them. And those who did have jobs and wanted to save for the future had no place to put their savings. All the existing banks were commercial or merchant banks at that time.

Thus at a meeting at the City Hotel on November 29, 1816, a group of well-to-do New Yorkers led by John Pintard, DeWitt Clinton, and Thomas Eddy adopted a plan to found a savings bank. It so happened that in Boston the Provident Institution for Savings had already opened that year, which may have spurred on these New Yorkers. Also Clinton in particular knew that the Erie Canal, which he was promoting, would need a great deal of private financing and that New Yorkers could only benefit if their savings were invested in the waterway. Also supporting a savings bank for New York was the Society for the Prevention of Pauperism, of which Eddy and Pintard were founders. In 1818 they opened a savings bank in the basement of the Almshouse, which was first called the Saving Fuel Fund Society and then the Bank for Savings when it was chartered by the state legislature on March 26, 1819. It opened for business on July 3, 1819, the first savings bank in New York and the second in the country.

At the first meeting of the Bank for Savings after it received a charter on April 5, 1819, John Pintard and Thomas Eddy were designated trustees, as was Major General Jonas Mapes together with other prominent New Yorkers such as William Bayard and Philip Hone. Mapes was perhaps the more popular member of the board of trustees, and he did have through the bank an acquaintanceship with all of the leaders of the city for much of his adult life.

The growth of deposits in the Bank for Savings was remarkable. Two weeks after its opening, $20,000 had been deposited. By the end of 1819 they had reached $153,000 from 1,527 depositors. Within five years it had 30,000 depositors with assets of $1.5 million and was the single largest holder of Erie Canal bonds. Soon many other savings banks would open: Seamen's, Greenwich, Bowery, and others.

After such a modest beginning in the basement of the Almshouse, the

Bank for Savings built and occupied its own building at 23 Chambers Street in 1825 and at 43 Chambers Street in 1829. Early presidents were William Bayard, John Pintard, and Philip Hone. The chief accountant was Daniel E. Tylee, General Mapes's brother-in-law and son of Tammany leader John Tylee. It was an important and long-lasting institution in the city and one of which General Mapes was proud to be a leader.

On July 1, 1817, DeWitt Clinton took his oath of office as governor of New York. And only three days later work began in Rome, New York, to build the Erie Canal. The two events were closely linked in the history of the state. Historian John Seelye said, "Second only perhaps to the Constitution, the Erie Canal was a premier creation of the Enlightenment in America."[51] And the person most responsible for this notable accomplishment was surely De-Witt Clinton. Historian Doris Kearns Goodwin confirms this opinion: "The pioneering New York Governor had opened opportunities for all New York-ers and left a permanent imprint on the state when he persuaded the Legislature to support the Erie Canal project."[52] The planning for such a canal had begun many years earlier.

Clinton's support for a canal between the Hudson River and Lake Erie, a distance of about 360 miles, began in 1810 when he joined with Gouverneur Morris, Thomas Eddy, Philip Schuyler, and Jonas Platt, all Federalists, to propose it to the state legislature. After being named a canal commissioner he traveled its length with surveyors and engineers before presenting a report that proposed construction of a continuous waterway from Albany to Lake Erie at a cost of five million dollars. The concept was approved but not the money. Clinton and Morris were sent to Washington to ask President Madison for federal help, only to be refused. By then the War of 1812 intervened and the Erie Canal project had to wait. Clinton went back to being mayor of New York.

After leaving the mayoralty in 1815, Clinton again worked hard to promote the project and to raise private funds from businesses that would benefit the most. They were very enthusiastic. Momentum began to build, and in spite of initial opposition from Tammany Hall, the pro-Clinton faction won out with legislative approval in April 1817 for a July groundbreaking of the state-owned, state-financed, state-run enterprise. It was called by many "Clinton's ditch."

The Erie Canal was described as follows: "363-miles long, 40-feet wide at water level narrowing to 28 feet wide at the bottom, and four-feet deep. The canal rose and descended a distance of 660 feet through 83 massive locks and passed over 18 aqueducts."[53] Goods were transported in special flat-bottomed canal barges, towed by horses at first before the use of steam became prevalent, along a course that generally followed the Mohawk River valley. It was built by engineers and laborers, many of whom were German, Irish, and Welsh immigrants. The canal was completed in eight years, two less than had been scheduled. An average trip from Buffalo to New York on the canal and thus down the Hudson took about ten days, slightly longer on return because of the water current. It transformed commerce in the northeast, assured New York City's claim to being the largest city in the nation for well over a century, and immediately spurred on the building of many more canals throughout the land.

With the Erie Canal under way, another step in the progress of democracy was taken in New York State in 1821 with the call for a constitutional convention. The rules for the governance of the state had not been changed in a major way since they were established in 1777, except for minor adjustments in 1804 when suffrage requirements had been lowered. Since then the population of the state had increased dramatically, and with the end of the War of 1812, the Federalist party had pretty much disappeared in New York. By 1821 the dominant Democratic Party was split between those who looked to Governor De-Witt Clinton as the leader and those who were rallying around upstate lawyer Martin Van Buren. Included in the latter group were the city Tammanyites who considered Clinton an aristocrat. The recession in 1819 also heightened demand for political reform, as under the old constitution three quarters of the city's male population could not vote for governor or state senator and one third could not vote for congressmen or assemblymen. Of course, women could not vote at all. Clearly a change in suffrage rules was sorely needed.

On March 13, 1821, the state legislature provided for a referendum to be held at the annual election in April on the question of whether or not to hold a special convention to revise the state constitution; should the vote be favorable, that the number of delegates be the same as the number of assemblymen in the state to be chosen at a special election in the third week of June; and finally that these delegates should assemble at Albany on the last Tuesday in August to begin their deliberations. Any changes made by the convention were also to be confirmed by a referendum of voters.

The reform movement in the state was led by Van Buren and the Tammanyites, who sensed their chance to gain control of the political process from Governor Clinton, who mistakenly resisted change. He feared that with the end of any constraints on all-white-male suffrage, which radicals were demanding, he would lose the next election and his power in the state. At the next regular election on April 24, the voters did authorize a special convention just as Clinton had feared. By the following June the delegates were chosen and he had lost control of the whole process. The convention assembled on August 28th to begin its work. "Everything wears an auspicious appearance," wrote a delegate, Odgen Edwards, who was counsel to the Common Council of New York City. Daniel D. Tompkins, former governor of New York and then vice president of the United States, was chosen to preside. He was considered neutral between the Clintonites and the Tammany–Van Buren faction. The convention would meet for two and a half months to accomplish the important task, longer than it took the delegates in 1787 to write the Constitution of the United States.

The delegates had been at work for less than a week when a huge distraction occurred that caused some of them to return to their homes. On September 3, New York City, Brooklyn, and Queens were struck by a tropical hurricane. Called "a tremendous gale" at the time, the storm would now be considered a hurricane based on the report of damage sustained. The *New York Evening Post* reported as follows:

> *A 'Tremendous gale' strikes New York causing much damage.*
>
> When the gale was at its height it presented a most awful spectacle. The falling of slate from the roofs of buildings, and broken glass from windows, made it unsafe for any one to venture into the streets.... The tide, although low water when the gale commenced, rose to an unusual height, overflowing all the wharves and filling cellars of all the stores on the margin of the East and North rivers. Great quantities of lumber, and other property on the wharves, have either been floated off or been damaged....
>
> The wharves on the North river are all injured, the frame work being generally started from the foundation.... The Steam Boat dock at Market field street is destroyed. The Battery is partly inundated, the earth washed away as far as the first row of trees, and the lamps in front of the Flag staff, together with the benches, all carried away.... The wharves on the East river were very much injured, some

entirely destroyed—all so much so that its dangerous for carts to venture on them. . . .

Some houses were unroofed and blown over, in the upper part of the city. One in Broadway, near the Lead Factory was blown down and killed ten cows. . . . A number of trees were prostrated in the Park. . . . The brick bats, tile, slates, lead, &c. from the tops of houses, and limbs of trees, were flying in every direction. A man was struck by a sign board in the Bowery, and had his arm broken—The Bloomingdale Road we understand is almost impassable by the falling of trees. Besides this, five boats were destroyed and eight injured in the wharves of the city, about ten chimneys were blown down, and many ships in the harbour were damaged.[54]

When the delegates returned to Albany to resume deliberations, they were faced with difficult and far-reaching decisions. There was widespread agreement to remove both the Council of Revision and the Council of Appointment, and to give to local voters the choice of most local officials. The only exception was that the office of mayor of New York would be an appointment by the city's Common Council. The mayor would not be elected by voters until 1834, when Cornelius W. Lawrence was elected.* The issue of suffrage was much more contentious.

After weeks of debate between the upstate landed gentry led by Chancellor James Kent, who wanted no change, and Tammany radicals who wanted an immediate end to all constraints on white male suffrage, a compromise was reached. Led by Martin Van Buren, the moderates proposed that suffrage be conferred on all 21-year-old white males who had lived in their districts for six months and had either paid taxes, served in the militia, or worked on the roads.

---

* On April 25, 1833, the state legislature approved a constitutional amendment providing for a popular election of mayor in the city of New York. This amendment was ratified by voters the following November by a very large majority. The first election under the new rules was set for the three days of April 8–10, 1834. As candidates, the committee of National Republicans nominated former congressman Gulian C. Verplanck, and the Tammany Democrats chose (after their first choice declined to run) Cornelius W. Lawrence, the present congressman and a supporter of President Andrew Jackson. It was a close and bitter contest during which disturbances were so serious that the militia had to be called out to restore order. A total of 35,141 voters cast their ballots in this first mayoralty election, and Lawrence won by 179. However, the Whigs (successor to the Federalists) elected a majority of the Common Council, giving a balance to city government.

This modest restriction on white male suffrage lasted only for five years, when, in 1826, a constitutional amendment removed all restrictions on white males 21 years or older. New York became a democracy for white males in that year.

The Constitutional Convention adjourned on November 10 when 98 out of its 106 delegates signed their names in approval of the new constitution. In addition to the matter of suffrage, other changes were in the powers of appointment. Common councils would appoint local offices such as mayors, justices, and clerks, and the state legislature would appoint state judges. Also the duration of the governor's term was shortened to two years from three. Generally speaking, the people received more power through the legislatures at the expense of executive and judicial functions of government. On January 15, 1822, the voters (under the former constitution) impressively endorsed the new one at the polls.

Not all were happy with the change. Former Federalists such as Peter Jay, James Kent, and Governor DeWitt Clinton feared that they would become more in the minority and that business would suffer. Clinton, facing defeat in 1822, withdrew from the governor's race. His fortunes, however, would improve again, thanks to the Erie Canal. Politically the winner was Martin Van Buren and of course Tammany Hall. The former went on to become governor of New York, vice president and then president of the United States, and the latter began a very extended control of New York City politics, backed by all the male Irish immigrants that could vote after they had been in New York six months. The new constitution discriminated against persons of color. Not even mentioned in the old one, they had to meet a higher standard in the new, a more rigid test of residence and property holding. In 1826, out of a population of 13,000 in New York City, only 16 persons of color were qualified to vote. The voting roles were made up of white males only.

New York's first trade school—designed to teach useful skills—was established in 1820 when the General Society of Mechanics and Tradesmen founded an Apprentices' Library on Chatham Street. In April of the following year, the Common Council granted them a 60-year lease on property on Chambers Street for the building of a school that opened its doors on November 26, 1821 and continued to be used until 1858, when a larger space became necessary. The school was a particular interest of Elizabeth Mapes's Tylee siblings, some of whom had been leather merchants like her father.

Epidemics had been the scourge of New York and other cities since early colonial times. Typhus from Europe, smallpox, malaria, and yellow fever from the tropics came with great regularity as the city grew in size, causing higher death tolls. In 1798 an epidemic of yellow fever had struck New Yorkers, although no one knew of its cause or how it spread. In the nineteenth century there had been yellow fever epidemics in 1803 and in 1819. The latter had lasted for six weeks during September and early October, typical of the time of year when yellow fever spread.

On August 3, 1822, several cases of yellow fever were noted as having broken out on Rector Street near Trinity Church, and the board of health advised all persons residing in that vicinity to move away. It appeared that a new epidemic was under way. It was the custom at that time to require that areas be vacated when cases appeared, as it was assumed that the contagion was passed from person to person and that the cause was uncleanliness in the area of outbreak. Areas ordered closed were fenced off with wooden barricades after all buildings had been boarded up to protect personal property inside. In spite of these actions the disease began to spread. By August 23 the board of health expanded the closed-off area to include all buildings south of Trinity Church, including the customs house, the activities of which were moved uptown to Greenwich. The post office, the banks, the insurance offices, and the printing offices were also all moved uptown. The Common Council forbid burials in Trinity Cemetery and on August 30 banned all religious services in both Trinity Church and St. Paul's Chapel on Fulton Street. New York was fast becoming a city under siege. The governor ordered the state militia on duty to protect property that had been abandoned because of the epidemic.

On September 4 the board of health again expanded the closed off area to all buildings south of City Hall, but at the same time, fearing panic, stated "that all that part of the city north and east of City Hall, which contains three-fourths of the population, is perfectly healthy, and may be frequented with the utmost safety."[55] None of the measures taken so far were having any effect whatsoever on the spread of yellow fever, and it was estimated that upward of 50,000 people had been required to move out of the city.

On September 14 the board of health tried a new experiment, desperate to slow down the epidemic. They ordered that lime, charcoal, tanners bark, and ashes be placed on the streets and on burial grounds during the night "to disinfect the atmosphere in the lower part of the city."[56] Some streets were covered with lime, others with other types of disinfectant. However, even these extremely costly measures were having no effect. Week after week it only grew worse.

In response to a petition by clergy in the city, October 11 was chosen to be a day of "public humiliation and prayer in order to implore the Supreme ruler of the Universe to Stay the disease now prevailing among us... and in his infinite mercy to restore health to the City."[57] And perhaps that had an effect, because on October 26 an early black frost appeared, and from past experience people knew that meant the epidemic was nearing its end.

With this first frost fear vanished and the Common Council ordered that citizens could return to their homes after they had "cleaned and aired them thoroughly." An observer noted that, "the consequent numerous removals back to the city, resembled the breaking up of the camp of some large army."[58] The final toll for the three-month yellow fever epidemic was 401 cases diagnosed, of which 230 were fatal—a death rate of 57 percent. The city returned to its normal busy life after a time of great hardship when its economic life came to a standstill, for no ships landed or departed while the epidemic lasted.

A month later Mayor Stephen Allen presented to the council several recommendations, all of which made great sense to the people of the city. Some of these were to clean up the filth in the streets, find a better supply of clean water, establish a public hospital away from the heart of the city for diseased patients, and to keep the atmosphere as clean as possible. Unfortunately it would not be until 1900 that Walter Reed proved that the carrier of this plague was the mosquito and only its elimination could prevent the spread of this disease. Although worthy goals, the measures taken in the early nineteenth century had no effect on yellow fever.

The epidemic of 1822 was not the last to occur in New York. Soon even more deadly ones—cholera, typhus, and typhoid fever, the so-called immigrant diseases, which came with ships from Europe all through the rest of the nineteenth century—devastated New York and other port cities.

While the yellow fever epidemic was filling New York City with fear bordering on panic, Jonas and Elizabeth Mapes's daughter, Catherine Deliverance Adeline, was married to Jonas's apprentice, Victor Bicker Waldron. The ceremony at St. John's Church was presided over by the Reverend Mr. Doane. It is not known why they chose October 15 as the date to marry. They had

FULTON STREET AND MARKET

An aquatint by William J. Bennett. The Fulton Market on the right was erected in 1821.
For much of his working life, Mapes was located two or three blocks north of this site on Pearl
and then on Water Street. He represented the Second Ward on the Common Council.

SOUTH STREET FROM MAIDEN LANE

Aquatint by William J. Bennett 1834. A forest of masts lined South Street belonging to vessels
from around the world in the 1820s. General Mapes's tailor shop was located on
31 Wall Street in that period and was very profitable.

known each other since they were young children, as Victor was the son of John Waldron, who had taught Jonas the tailor's trade after he had come to the city in 1788. Adeline was 22 and Victor was 24 when they married. He was already following in his father-in-law's path as a merchant tailor and member of the state militia, which he had joined in 1818. In 1821 he had been promoted to captain in the 142nd Regiment and was the paymaster. The 142nd was the regiment General Mapes had commanded in 1812 before his promotion. After a year as paymaster, Victor became an aide-de-camp for his father-in-law. In any event, the young couple chose to marry possibly because they all had to leave their home at 56 Broad Street, which was inside the "infectious" zone of the yellow fever epidemic. They most likely lived with the thousands of others in temporary shelters to the north for the three months it lasted. Also they wanted to start a family. Victor and Adeline's first child was a daughter, born in 1823 at 40 Pine Street, the new Mapes home. They named her Elizabeth Eglantine after her maternal grandmother, Elizabeth Mapes. Their second child, also a daughter, arrived two years later in 1825 and was christened Caroline Amanda. Three more would follow.

Mapes's business, Mapes, Oakley, and Company, had just moved from Water Street to 31 Wall Street and had been established for less than a year at the new address when the yellow fever struck in August 1822. It was an inauspicious beginning at the new location. Also located in the "infectious" zone, it had to close down with most of New York for the duration. When it reopened in November the partnership had changed to Mapes, Son, and Waldron. Oakley had departed and General Mapes had asked his eldest son, Charles, and his son-in-law Victor B. Waldron to join him as partners. Jonas, his wife, and Charles lived at 56 Broad Street. The newlyweds Adeline and Victor lived at 10 State Street. The following year the Mapeses moved to 40 Pine Street,* where the Waldrons joined them for the remainder of General Mapes's life. All of these locations were close by his business at 31 Wall Street.

From the time Mapes, Son, and Waldron opened in 1822 until well after the general's death when it became Mapes and Waldron, New York City was experiencing a huge boom lasting a full 15 years. The business of tailoring for

---

* Pine Street was a residential street until 1831–34, when most houses were torn down and replaced with commercial structures.

men was changing as well during that time. Whereas a Broadway clothier or tailor had previously hung samples of his ready-mades outside his shop, competition from clothing made in London began to appear in the windows of tailor shops in New York. Englishmen began to set up their own clothing shops and offer tailoring services. In 1825, Aaron Arnold opened a shop on Pine Street offering "silks, woolens, laces, and shawls from Europe and the Orient." In 1830 James Constable became his partner and they opened uptown as Arnold Constable, the first modern emporium. In 1826, Englishman Samuel Lord and his partner George Washington Taylor opened a store on Catherine Street called Lord and Taylor. Gradually the tailoring business became limited to alterations as the department stores became more and more successful.

During this time imports into the port of New York grew from 38 percent of the nation's total in 1821 to 62 percent in 1836. On a single day in 1824, 324 ships were at anchor in the Upper Bay of New York waiting to find a wharf at which to dock. The Cotton Triangle was also well established by then. Ships laden with the valuable commodity would sail from New Orleans to New York, where it was transferred to an eastbound ship to Liverpool, which had just made the westbound passage with immigrants and European cargo. The Port of New York handled not only the cargo of cotton but also the insurance, interest, commissions, and freight changes on the transaction. In 1822, cotton accounted for 40 percent of New York's domestic imports, all on its way to English looms. Flour was a distant second.

During the 15-year boom, New York's population leaped ahead from 124,000 (1820) to 200,000 (1830) to 270,000 by 1835, becoming the fastest-growing city in the country. The population of every ward tripled or quadrupled, causing crowding, congestion, and soaring prices. The value of land in Manhattan went from $65 million dollars to over $143 million dollars and then up to $233 million in the next 12 months, enabling landowning families to amass huge fortunes. These were led by John Jacob Astor but also included many old Knickerbocker names such as Livingston, Stuyvesant, Roosevelt, Rhinelander, Bayard, Goelet, Cutting, and others. To have owned real estate during the 1820s almost ensured a fortune to the landlord.

CHAPTER ELEVEN

Lafayette's Return

1824–25

The year 1824 marked the fortieth year since Evacuation Day, when all British troops left New York at the end of the American Revolution. To celebrate that occasion, the only surviving major general of that war was invited to return to America for a visit. On the morning of August 15, the packet ship *Cadmus*, 31 days out of Le Havre, arrived at the Narrows slightly ahead of schedule and was greeted by a thirteen-gun salute—one gun for each of the original thirteen states of the Union. After docking at Staten Island, the ship's distinguished visitor came ashore to spend the night at the home of Vice President Daniel D. Tompkins. In the French custom he had seven names but was known to almost all Americans as the Marquis de Lafayette, the man who first came to the United States in 1777 and, with the support of his own country, turned the tide in the War of Independence. Over the next 13 months, at the age of 67, he would visit the 24 states of the country, meeting old comrades and making journeys to places he had known forty years before. Everywhere he went, he was royally received and feted. He was a symbol of good will and solidarity between America and France.

New York had been preparing for Lafayette's visit for several months, and as the economic boom continued, New Yorkers were in a mood to celebrate their own success as well as the arrival of their guest. The committee for the reception of the marquis and his party—including his son George Washington Lafayette and a servant—had taken rooms at the City Hotel on Broadway, the city's finest at that time. They endeavored to avoid too much pomp, for "vain and ostentatious ceremonies would be equally unacceptable to our republican habits. There are occasions, however, when the American people choose to pour forth their feelings in acts of unrestrained hospitality, munificence and even profusion. Such will be the case when the Marquis arrives in our City."[59] It must be observed that "republican habits" were suppressed during the marquis's visit to New York.

The visit officially began at nine A.M. on the morning of August 16, when the marquis boarded the steamboat *Chancellor Livingston* for the trip across the Upper Bay from Staten Island to the Battery. A flotilla of steamboats, at least two frigates, and hundreds of sailing craft followed in procession. Amid salutes from the harbor forts he disembarked at Castle Garden to be greeted by the cheers of nearly 50,000 people. The *New York Evening Post* described the occasion: "The ringing of bells, the roar of the cannon, the display of the national standard at all the public places, the decoration of the steam boats and shipping with the flags of every nation, the martial strains of music, and the shouts of the multitudes, proclaimed that it was a jubilee which could not fail to be enjoyed by every true friend of liberty. Escorted by the militia and the Cincinnati, the marquis proceeded to City Hall where he was welcomed by Mayor Paulding and introduced to members of the Common Council. The portrait room was placed at his disposal during his residence in the city. After this reception he retired to his apartments in the City Hotel, and dined there with the corporation. In the evening, buildings were illuminated, and the theatres, public gardens, etc. displayed transparencies and fireworks."[60] Not since the inauguration of George Washington as president on April 30, 1789, had there been such a festive day in the city.

Among the many stops made in the city by Lafayette during his visit were inspections of the military posts. During these he was accompanied by officers of the state militia, including Major Generals Mapes, Morton, Clarkson, Fish, and Fleming. All of these generals had defended their city during the War of 1812 and proudly showed the marquis various fortifications, including the Brooklyn Navy Yard, the forts in the Upper Bay, and, on September 8, Fort Lafayette on the Brooklyn side of the Narrows, where a dinner was held in his honor.

During the first of the marquis's New York visits from August 16 to August 20 (there would be three more during his stay in America), he was received in City Hall by the Society of the Cincinnati (General Washington's officers and their male descendants); sat for a portrait at the request of the Common Council; received a delegation from Baltimore with resolutions and letters; received 300 members of the New York Bar; and gave a dinner for Captain Rodgers and the naval officers in New York. Rodgers was the port naval commander at the time.

Lafayette and his party left for Boston by steamship on August 20, to return again on September 5. Meanwhile in New York, planning continued for the next fortnight, which would conclude with what came to be known as "the Grand Fete to LaFayette" to be held at Castle Garden off the Battery. An overflow crowd was expected of about 6,000 guests. A miniature head of the marquis, engraved by Asher B. Durand, was being stamped on souvenirs, watch ribbons, belts, gloves and other articles of apparel to be worn on the great evening. The program for the event listed the names of the many managers of the fete and included the five New York generals, Mapes, Morton, Clarkson, Fish, and Fleming.

Upon his return on September 5, the marquis was entertained the next day, his 67th birthday, with a dinner at Washington Hall. This was followed by a visit to Columbia College (still located near City Hall). On September 9 he was guest of honor at a grand oratorio by the New York Choral Society in St. Paul's Chapel, at the end of which the choir sang "La Marseillaise."

The Grand Fete had been planned for the evening of September 10, but bad New York weather forced two postponements. While waiting, Lafayette received a sword from the Ninth Regiment, was honored at dinner by the French residents of the city, and received several degrees of masonry by the Society of Freemasons.

Finally, clear weather arrived on September 14. The reception and subscription ball took place at Castle Garden, called Castle Clinton until its recent acquisition by the city from the federal government.* It was connected to the Battery by a wooden bridge to which for this occasion carriages were allowed to drive. James Fenimore Cooper, the noted author, described its decoration: "The area with the walls was covered by a vast awning made of the sails of a ship-of-the-line and this was draped with flags. There

---

* Castle Clinton had been built in 1808 as a harbor fort when fears of a British invasion were great. It was called the West Battery until 1815.

were six thousand guests, a number that is rarely exceeded at any European entertainment, proof that established orders in society are not at all necessary for the tranquility of its ordinary intercourse." He then tells of the arrival of Lafayette on the scene: "The music changed to a national air, the gay sets dissolved as by a charm and the dancers . . . formed a lane whose sides were composed of masses that might have contained two thousand eager faces each. Through this gay multitude the old man slowly passed, giving and receiving the most cordial and affectionate salutations at every step. . . . To me he appeared some venerable and much respected head of a vast family who had come to pass an hour amid their gay and innocent revels. He was like a father awing his children."[61]

Mary Mapes Dodge, the Mapes's granddaughter, years later remembered being shown by her Grandma Mapes—who, as wife of the welcoming general, danced with Lafayette at the ball—the satin slippers she had worn on that occasion. She wrote:

> Grandma told me all about it,
> Told me so I couldn't doubt it,
> How she danced—my Grandma danced,
> Long ago . . . [62]

At two o'clock in the morning Lafayette, his son, and their party left the ball, went directly to the steamboat *James Kent* and departed New York for a trip up the Hudson to visit Albany and other towns along the river. After six days along the Hudson River he returned to New York City for four more days before departing for a visit to the south. His departure was also marked with ceremony, being escorted to the wharf by Mayor Paulding, the Common Council, the Cincinnati cavalry, infantry and a salute by the artillery. Since his arrival in New York on August 16 until his departure on September 23, the marquis had managed only a few days of rest, and the United States tour had only just started. It would be more than nine months later before he returned again to the city. During this interval a new street had been opened and named Lafayette Place.

On May 11, 1825, the Common Council invited the marquis and his party to come to New York for the celebration of the Fourth of July that year. He accepted the invitation and arrived after a trip over many of the completed sections of the new Erie Canal between Buffalo and Albany, where he was royally greeted at every stop.

In New York City on July 4 the *New York Spectator* describes that busy day:

> The celebration of this Fourth of July is particularly memorable because of the presence of Lafayette. Received at 10 A.M. in the governor's room of the city hall by a committee of the common council, he is conducted to the council chamber where he receives an address by the Lieutenant Governor Talmadge on behalf of the senate and people of the state. In front of the city hall he received the "marching salute" of a military and firemen's parade. He listened to an oration by the Rev. Dr. Cummings in the Middle Dutch Church, and in the afternoon visited the Society of the Cincinnati to walk with them at 5 o'clock to partake of the corporation dinner in the "banqueting room of the City Hall." In the evening, attended by a committee of the revolutionary officers and citizens, he visited the Park Theatre, and at 10 o'clock repaired to Castle Garden, where 8,000 persons greeted him, and witnessed a display of fireworks.

Ten days later Lafayette left New York for a second tour to the South, ending at Washington D.C., where on September 7 he boarded the U.S. frigate *Brandywine* for the trip home to France. It could not have been a coincidence that almost exactly 48 years earlier, in September 1777, he had first come to America to fight with the patriots at the Battle of Brandywine in Delaware.

The welcoming committee chaired by William Bayard had devised a busy schedule that both honored Lafayette and showed off the city to its best advantage. Each of his three visits demonstrated that huge crowds of people could assemble peacefully to honor the hero and that New York had not forgotten the cause of constitutional republicanism. As Cadwallader Colden said, "An exhibition of bayonets is not essential to the preservation of order in New York."[63]

CHAPTER TWELVE

"The Wedding of the Waters"
Clinton and the Erie Canal, 1825

After being out of office for two years DeWitt Clinton's political fortunes began to improve, primarily because of his continuing connection with and support of the Erie Canal, which by the summer of 1825 was nearing completion. In the fall of 1824 he had again run for governor and had been reelected to succeed Judge Joseph C. Yates, who had served only one term. Clinton was associated with the canal more than any other individual, and his return to office put him in a position to oversee its final completion and the ceremonies surrounding its opening.

The focus of these ceremonies was to be a voyage by a flat-bottomed canal boat named *Seneca Chief* from Buffalo, on Lake Erie, through the canal to Albany, where it would enter the Hudson River and proceed down river to Sandy Hook, on the Atlantic Ocean. *Seneca Chief* was a boat of only four feet draught, as that was the maximum depth of the canal at some places on the route. It was estimated that the voyage would take ten days with many stops along the way for ceremonies and speeches.

Planning in New York City for its part of the ceremonies began on September 12 when William Bayard, Cadwallader Colden, and John Pintard, on behalf of the city's merchants and chamber of commerce, asked the Common Council to appoint a committee to develop plans to commemorate this important event in the history of New York. Two weeks later the committee of 15 leading citizens reported that it had held its first meeting and that Richard

Riker, council recorder, had accepted the chair. Other members included: William Bayard for the merchants and chamber of commerce; Major General J. Morton, Artillery Division; Major General J. Mapes, Second Infantry Division; R.E. Mount for the Societies (charitable organizations); Charles Rhind for the Aquatic Committee; and Augustus Fleming, grand marshall for the day. This would be General Mapes's last public appearance at a city function before his death in July 1827.

The mayor asked the planning committee to host the celebration on behalf of New York City. The list of guests was vast and included the president of the United States, the vice president, and all federal, state, and local officials of New York and neighboring states. By October 4 all of the arrangements by committees representing Buffalo, Albany, and New York had been agreed upon. The voyage was set to start on October 26 along a canal that was 363 miles long (to Albany), 40 feet wide, four feet deep, rising and descending 660 feet over that distance through 83 stone locks and passing over 18 aqueducts along the way.

On the appointed day, Governor Clinton with several dignitaries boarded *Seneca Chief* in Buffalo for the eastbound journey. Also on board were symbols of the western lands from which the waters of the Great Lakes flowed: maple boards from Ohio, whitefish from the Great Lakes, an Indian canoe from Lake Superior, and a small wooden barrel decorated with an American bald eagle and the words "Water" and "Lake Erie" inscribed in gold. The barrel of water was to be emptied into the Atlantic Ocean off Sandy Hook, symbolizing the "wedding of the waters," the name given to the event.

Seneca Chief together with several other barges and sloops departed along the canal toward Albany, stopping along the way at small towns for many speeches, parades, and feasts. At Albany they were treated to a great banquet for 600 people at the city's boat basin before heading down the Hudson River for New York, accompanied by a squadron of eight steamboats. On November 4 this "aquatic procession" as it was called, arrived off Fort Gansevoort (Greenwich Village today) at six A.M., then proceeded to the Battery for the start of what was described as "one of the most spectacular celebrations in the city's history."[64] They began with a welcome by the mayor and the Common Council from the steamboat *Washington* and a response from Governor Clinton from the steamboat *Chancellor Livingston* off the Battery. Clinton said in part: "Standing near the confines of the ocean, and now connected by navigable communications with the Great Lakes of the North and the West, there will be no limit to your lucrative extensions of trade and commerce. The valley of the Mississippi will soon pour its treasures into this great emporium through the channels now formed and forming, and wherever wealth is to be acquired or enterprise can be attempted the power and capacity of your city will be felt, and its propitious influence on human happiness will be acknowledged."[65] The governor was accurately describing the future of New York City in these prescient remarks.

The flotilla then proceeded up the East River to the Navy Yard, where officers of the navy boarded *Washington* before all vessels headed down the Bay through the Narrows to Sandy Hook. There they formed a circle of about three miles for the ceremony of uniting the waters of Lake Erie to the Atlantic Ocean. Amid the decorated ships on which bands played while guns from the shore fired salutes, Governor Clinton poured water from the cask into the sea sealing the "wedding of the waters" forever. The entire flotilla then returned to the Battery at about three o'clock for the next phase of the day, the grand procession through the streets of Manhattan.

Some 7,000 marchers joined in the parade, lined up in ranks according to occupations or professions. Among these were lawyers, physicians, militia, firemen, artisans, craftsmen, and journeymen's societies (early labor unions), among them the Tailors and Journeymen Tailors Society of which General Mapes was prominent. The route of march from the Battery was up Greenwich Street to Canal Street, over to Broadway, up to Broome Street and across to the Bowery, down to Pearl Street, down to the Battery again, and then up to Broadway to City Hall. It was thought that more than 100,000 people, two thirds of the population of the city, witnessed this extraordinary procession, the largest gathering of people in North America up to that time.

As darkness fell upon the city, the host committee had asked that all buildings be illuminated. Therefore at 7:00 P.M., beginning with City Hall, which was lighted with hundreds of wax candles and oil lamps, all the city lights came on, presenting a dazzling spectacle. At 10:00 festivities concluded for the day with a display of fireworks in City Hall Park, seen by thousands elbow to elbow in front of New York's most elegant building.

Three days later, on November 7, a Grand Canal Ball concluded events for the celebration. It was held in a building known as the Lafayette Circus,

VIEWS OF THE ERIE CANAL

A watercolor drawing by J. W. Hill gives a good idea of the charm and fascination of travel in these inland waterways. The Erie Canal was opened with a celebration in the autumn of 1825 that was planned and hosted by a committee including General Mapes. It was his last official function for his city.

which had been connected to the building behind it to form a 180-foot-long space. The circus had been a riding school on what is now called West Broadway. It was fitted up for the ball with great splendor to become the largest public space in the city. The total cost for all these events came to $19,648 according to council records.

A day earlier the barge *Seneca Chief* had been towed up the Hudson by a steamboat to Albany, where it entered the canal for the return trip to Buffalo. On board this time was another keg, this one filled with salt water from the Atlantic. Inscribed in green letters was "Neptune's Return to Pan."

No one fully foresaw the enormous benefits that the Erie Canal would bring to New York City as well as to all the towns from Buffalo east along its path. In fact, its benefits to the young nation in 1825 were just as great. It was by far the most important project undertaken to spur economic development and westward expansion in the United States. It inspired the digging of canals all over the country. It changed the course of westward migration of people. After 1825 the traveler from Philadelphia to Pittsburgh went by way of New York, Albany, Buffalo and then took the wagon road down to Pittsburgh. It was cheaper and quicker than over the Allegheny Mountains. Towns changed almost overnight. Troy, New York, became one of the nation's most important industrial centers for its production of iron before the Civil War.

For New York itself, already in a boom after 1820, the Erie Canal increased and extended that boom until 1837. Erie boatmen were steering 42 barges a day through the canal to New York City within its first year of operation. Shipping costs declined from one hundred dollars a ton to under nine dollars a ton. Enough money came in to the state's coffers in tolls to pay for its cost of construction in one year and subsidize 600 miles of other canals in the state in the years to come. A trio of "anthracite coal" canals funneled that precious fuel from Pennsylvania to Manhattan, giving the city cheap energy for rapid expansion. The value of land in Manhattan rose from $65 million in 1826 to $88 million in 1830 to over $143 million in 1835, more than twice as much in less than ten years. The population grew from 167,000 in 1825 to 270,000 in 1835, fed largely by immigration from Ireland and Germany.

Shipbuilding and shipping were expanding as well. During 1824, 65 vessels, 17 of which were steamboats, were built in the Port of New York. The largest builder was the firm of Brown and Bell. By 1825, 16 packet ships (still all sail) made the transatlantic run to Liverpool in Great Britain and four went to Le Havre in France. Ships also departed from Belfast, Dublin, and Cork in Ireland, bound for New York, Boston, and Philadelphia, carrying immigrants. To provide for those who remained in New York new wards were added. By 1825 there were eleven wards below 14th Street and Ward Twelve above that double-width street. Tammany Hall grew in size and political influence, as did majorities in the Democratic Party.

General Mapes had lived during his last years under favorable economic condition, and the area surrounding his Pine Street home was becoming increasingly commercial. His tailoring shop on Wall Street was being looked after by his son Charles and his son-in-law Victor Waldron. The center of residential life was moving north along Broadway and on the streets running off it. St. John's Park in particular (Hudson Square today) had become a fashionable residential area developed by Trinity Church, which owned the land as part of the Queen's farm, a grant of 1705. Had Jonas Mapes been a younger man he likely would have moved to one of these areas. Many new buildings had been completed in Manhattan by 1827. Most prominent was the elegant Merchants Exchange, designed by Martin E. Thompson, on the south side of Wall Street, east of Mapes's shop. It had replaced the Tontine Coffee House as the home of the New York Stock Exchange and housed trading of all kinds of goods. Also in that year the dry-goods house of Arnold, Constable & Co. was founded by Aaron Arnold on Canal Street. It was the first of its kind in the city and would soon become a notable department store known around the country. It was stores such as Arnold, Constable and Lord and Taylor that supplied clothing for customers and put the merchant tailors out of business.

The year 1827 did not bring only favorable news. On January 15, the *New York Evening Post* reported that smallpox had so spread that the Common Council directed the physicians of the city to call at every house and to vaccinate every person willing to "submit to the operation." With the large number of unvaccinated immigrants growing each year, controlling smallpox was a discouraging task. Many were afraid to "submit" and the disease would spread.

On July 4, 1827—Emancipation Day—the owning of slaves in New York State became illegal. It was the last northern state, except for New Jersey, to end the lawful practice of enslaving human beings, although the segregation of free African-Americans would continue in the city for many years to come.

The process of changing the laws had begun in March 1799 when the state legislature provided that "any child born of a slave after the 4th of July next shall be deemed to be born free," requiring however that such child continue a servant until a certain age, as if it had been bound to service by the overseers of the poor. The owner of a slave was permitted to free the slave immediately. It was a very small start.

Eighteen years later, in March 1817, the legislature revised the act again by declaring that "every negro, mulatto, or mustee, within the state, born before the 4th of July 1799 shall be free after the 4th of July 1827; and that every child born of a slave within this state after July 4th, 1799 should be free but remain a servant of the owner of his or her mother, and be taught to read."[66]

Thus on July 4, 1827, Emancipation Day, all black churches in the city held services of prayer and thanksgiving for the freedom that had finally been given to their people. Ironically, for many freedom meant unemployment, no housing, even starvation, and at best segregation. "The rights of man are decided by the color of their skin," said the Reverend Peter Williams Jr.[67] Blacks were banned from cabins in the Hudson River boats, not allowed on street stages or the new omnibuses. They were also barred from all public schools and all private schools except one, the Quaker-run African Free School. Black women suffered as much as men, with service in homes being taken by the Irish immigrant population. Finally, all black males were excluded from voting, which was still a white male's privilege.

CHAPTER THIRTEEN

The Death of General Mapes

1827

Little is known of the final years of General Mapes's life. Upon his retirement from the New York State militia he was honored by the officers of the 142nd Regiment he had once commanded in the traditional manner with a dinner and a gift of a pair of silver pitchers. These he treasured and willed to his eldest son, Charles. As they are mentioned in his will written in April 1823, his retirement preceded that date. His son-in-law Victor B. Waldron was also given a silver pitcher when he retired in 1836 as colonel of the same regiment.[*]

General Mapes spent his last year in his house at 40 Pine Street with his wife, Elizabeth, their son Charles, their daughter Adeline and her husband, Victor, their son James, and two granddaughters, Elizabeth and Caroline Waldron. He died there on July 10, 1827, at the age of 59. In addition to his immediate family he was survived by his 83-year-old mother, Deliverance Hawkins Mapes, who, after the death of his father, had married a Mills and lived in Stony Brook, Long Island.

Jonas Mapes always had a close bond with his mother and would often visit her in Stony Brook, where she had lived for the many years since her

---

[*] This pitcher is in the possession of the author.

children had grown up and left the house she had with her husband James Mapes in Mattituck, Long Island.

Jonas Mapes was buried in the Mills family graveyard in Head of the Harbor, next to Stony Brook. The site was chosen by him undoubtedly at the request of his mother, who intended to be buried there next to her son, of whom she was especially proud. His gravestone reads: "In Memory of Major General Jonas Mapes who died July 10th, 1827, at 59 years 10 months." An inscription below is mostly indecipherable today except for the words "Loving the Lord." The plain white marble slab is placed flat on the ground (marked #21 in O'Berry's listing).

Directly opposite his grave is that of his mother. Her flat marble slab is inscribed: "In Memory of Deliverance Mills who died June 10th, 1829, in the 85th year of her age. Her life was useful and was long. Her friendship and affection strong" (marked #20 in O'Berry's listing).

In the same burial ground lie several Hawkinses: Deliverance's parents, Eleazer and Ruth Mills Hawkins; her sister, Ann Hawkins, who died at 16 years of age; and her brother Jonas Hawkins with his wife, Ruth Hawkins. Although it seems unusual to find General Mapes buried there, few cemeteries existed in Manhattan in 1827 and no other Mapes of that branch of his family was buried in the city until much later.

His younger son James later described his father as a man of dignity with a severity of countenance and carriage. From a humble start when as a young man he moved to newly freed New York City, Jonas Mapes joined both the New York State militia and the Merchant Tailors' Guild. In both careers he made his mark. He served his city as a major general as well as an elected alderman and provided for a family as a successful merchant tailor. Unlike some of his peers in that era he never accumulated significant wealth, but was able to provide comfortably for a family of four children and leave a business that would support two of them. He was a friend of the most significant New York figure of his era, Mayor and later Governor DeWitt Clinton. The two were born a year apart, married in the same year, and had nearby homes in Maspeth. Governor Clinton died in office in 1828 only six months after General Mapes's death. Happily both lived to see the success of the Erie Canal, which enabled New York City to remain the most important city in the nation.

Jonas Mapes signed his last will on April 4, 1823, adding a codicil on March 22, 1827. He died on July 10, 1827, and his will was proved on July 17. All took place in the City of New York, where he had lived since 1788, close to 40 years. In it he describes himself as a "Merchant Taylor," (using the old spelling of "tailor").

In the second paragraph he gives to his wife, Elizabeth Mapes, all his household furniture except the pair of silver pitchers from the officers of his regiment, which he gives to his oldest surviving child (Charles).

In the third paragraph he identifies his son Charles and his son-in-law Victor B. Waldron as his co-partners under the name of Mapes, Son, & Waldron, directing them to carry on the business on their own account by reorganizing the partnership, and "to return out of the firm a sum not exceeding Ten Thousand Dollars." Provided they shall deliver to Elizabeth Mapes a joint bond for the amount returned by them at the rate of six percent per annum, and they shall pay the balance of said co-partnership stock over and above said sum to be retained by them to his executors and executrix. (He offers his son and son-in-law up to $10,000 in a loan at six percent to run the tailor shop with the rest of his share of the firm going into his estate.)

In the fourth paragraph he authorizes his executors to sell or manage his real estate in any way they think proper with very broad powers.

In the fifth paragraph he authorizes his executors to loan his son James, when he is the age of 21, a sum not exceeding $5,000 to establish himself in the business. He must execute a bond for such amount at six percent per annum.

In the sixth paragraph he authorizes Elizabeth Mapes to appoint an agent to examine books of his estate and enjoins his executors to produce every record the agent requires.

In the seventh paragraph he says that the division of his estate shall be in accord with the laws of New York State in force for intestate estates.

Lastly, he nominates Elizabeth Mapes as executrix, Charles Mapes and Victor Waldron as executors. In the 1827 codicil he adds his son James, then 21 years old, as a fourth executor, as well as expressly stating that no son who

BROADWAY AND TRINITY CHURCH

A view looking south down Broadway from Liberty Street. A watercolor drawing by J. W. Hill. The Mapes and Waldron tailor shop had moved to 139 Broadway by 1831.

has been appointed executor of his will may be released from payment of monies he may owe his estate. This last codicil implies that Jonas may have loaned money to his sons and son-in-law to establish them as partners in the firm.[68]

Following Jonas Mapes's death in 1827, the new partnership, Mapes and Waldron, remained at 31 Wall Street until 1831, when it moved to 139 Broadway, an address much closer to the residential homes of the more affluent New Yorkers. It was located between Cedar Street and Liberty Street on the west side of Broadway. In the following year Charles Mapes left the business, so that Victor B. Waldron became the sole partner. He was 34 years old at the time. The move was well timed because in December 1835 the Great Fire consumed almost all of old Dutch New York south of Wall Street and east of Broad Street. Had the tailor shop still been at 31 Wall Street it would have been completely destroyed, whereas most of Broadway was saved. V. B. Waldron, merchant tailor, remained at 139 Broadway until 1842, when the opening of Union Square and 14th Street drew many customers to uptown New York. There is no listing of the tailor after his family moved uptown.

Jonas Mapes was survived by his wife, Elizabeth Tylee Mapes, who did not die until 1868 at the age of 91. She had been a widow for an extraordinary 41 years and survived both of her sons. During that long widowhood it was Grandma Mapes's custom to hold the family Christmas celebration at her home. Her granddaughter Mary Mapes (later Dodge) described it as follows:

> On Christmas it was grandma's custom to invite us all to dinner, and you may be sure every one who was invited went. It is strange to have to tell you our names—it seems as if you ought to know them. First there were mother and father, and Aunt Jane and Uncle Augustus; Allen and cousin Gus and Rosalie, and Louise and Lizzie and Sophy and Charley and Kate and Leslie and ever so many others—aunts, uncles, cousins, and relatives. And there was one stately great-uncle, of whom I now can remember only the shining gray circle of hair on top, a gorgeous bunch of seals dangling from beneath a big vest, and a pair of glossy boots below. I suppose there was more of him. Oh! Yes, there was a hand that came out very slowly and settled softly on our heads, with, "this is Jane Eliza's little one, eh!" or, "Well, Sophia, the little girl favors *you* most certainly. . . ."[69]

GRANDDAUGHTER MATILDA WALDRON ELDER (1834–1907)

On the left, with her daughter Louisine Waldron Elder (1855–1929) on the right.
A photograph by Emil Fr. Cassel in 1881

GRANDDAUGHTER MARY MAPES DODGE (1830–1905)

She was the author of *Hans Brinker; or the Silver Skates* and editor of *St. Nicholas Magazine* published by Charles Scribner and Sons.

The Mapes's eldest son, Charles, had married Addy Luff in 1824, and they had three sons: Charles, Daniel Tylee, and John Luff Mapes. Charles, like his father and, brother-in-law, joined the state militia. In 1835, after leaving the family firm of tailors, he became a paymaster in the U.S. Army. He died in 1852 at the age of 52.

The Mapes's daughter Adeline and Victor Waldron had a family of four daughters: Elizabeth Eglantine, Caroline Amanda, Louisine T., and Matilda Adelaide. A son, Charles, died in infancy. Adeline and Victor Waldron lived at several addresses downtown following Jonas Mapes's death. These were 75 William Street, 12 Duane Street, 51 Franklin Street, and 235 William Street. All four daughters were born at these downtown houses. In 1842 they moved uptown to 190 West 14th Street between 8th and 9th Avenues, living in a brownstone house across the street from one recently built by the successful sugar refiner Frederick C. Havemeyer Jr. It would be a fateful move by the Waldrons, intertwining those two families in the years to come. Victor B. Waldron died in 1848 at 50 years of age. Adeline died in 1878 at 78, a widow for thirty years, almost as long as her mother.

The Mapes's youngest son, James Jay, was educated at a classical school in Hempstead, Long Island, where in 1818–19 he was living with the English journalist and liberal reformer William Cobbett. Cobbett had spent those years in the United States writing his *Grammar of the English Language* and *Journal of a Year's Residence in the United States.* He undoubtedly influenced the twelve-year-old with his populist philosophy and interest in agriculture.

James grew up in a home where intellectual endeavors were valued more that material goods. He became a brilliant but impecunious, self-taught chemist, an inventor, and later a publisher. He became a professor of chemistry and natural philosophy at the National Academy of Design and the American Institute and introduced the use of chemical fertilizers in the country. Known as "Prof" or "the Professor" by students and colleagues alike, he lived in the worlds of both science and letters. Horace Greeley, founder of the *New York Tribune* and John Greenleaf Whittier, the poet, became close friends. Greeley especially was often in the Mapes home near the Battery. James was always experimenting, regardless of the cost, exercising an inventive mind that as a young boy would cause his father, the general, great annoyance.

His disregard for money would bring great pain to his family, his wife and his six children (two of whom were adopted). When he died in 1866 at the age of sixty, he left them deeply in debt with small prospects that it could be paid off. This burden fell to his talented daughter Mary Mapes Dodge to satisfy the obligations.

Mary, 36 when her father died, was already a widow with two sons of her own. Her husband, William Dodge, had been closer in age to her father than to her and had committed suicide in 1858. Shortly thereafter Mary began her brilliant career writing books for children, short stories at first and then in 1866 her classic, *Hans Brinker; or the Silver Skates*, which brought her great fame and, more important, money to pay off the family debts. *Brinker* became a worldwide success and was translated into many languages.

In 1873 Mary was asked by Charles Scribner and Sons to edit a new magazine for children, *St. Nicholas Magazine*. She was able to attract and hold writers such as Rudyard Kipling, Louisa May Alcott, and Mark Twain, making the magazine the most popular of its kind in America. She was certainly General Mapes's most famous grandchild. She died in 1905. Her father's debts had finally been settled.

The Mapes's youngest daughter, Catherine, married Charles L. Rhodes.

It is interesting to note the extraordinary longevity of the women who both preceded and followed General Mapes in his ancestral line.

Keziah Parshall Mapes 1707–82 (75 years)
Ruth Mills Hawkins 1721–1801 (80 years)
Deliverance Hawkins Mapes 1744–1829 (85 years)
Elizabeth Tylee Mapes 1777–1868 (91 years)
Adeline Mapes Waldron 1800–78 (78 years)
Matilda Waldron Elder 1835–1907 (72 years)

Between July 1827, when General Mapes died, and the end of 1828, New York City continued to grow and prosper. The city's center was moving uptown all the time, and by 1828 it was considered to be at City Hall, where the distinguished classical building stood at the north of a city park. Broadway was the grand boulevard and was described in the guidebook published by Andrew T. Goodrich that year as follows:

Broadway is the handsomest street, and the greatest thoroughfare in New York. It runs in a direct line from the Battery to Tenth Street, and is three miles in length, and 80 feet in breadth. It contains the principal retail shops of jewelers and watchmakers; also the principal book stores, merchant tailors [Victor B. Waldron moved to 139 Broadway in 1831], hatters, carpet and fancy dry good stores, confectioners, hotels, and boarding-houses; also four Episcopal Churches, and the hospital, the Masonic Hall, two museums, and the City Hall. It is well paved throughout, with the sidewalks 19-feet in width, laid with flagging stone. The perspective views in proceeding from the Battery up this street towards City Hall are striking to the eye of a stranger; we would notice especially the view standing by St. Paul's Church, and looking towards the north and northeast, as presenting the finest coup d'oeil in the city.[70]

Among the important buildings on Broadway was New York's oldest hotel, City Hotel, which needed refurbishment when 65-year-old John Jacob Astor purchased it in 1828. At the time he also owned the Park Theater and Vauxhall Gardens as well as the house called Richmond Hill and almost all the land along Greenwich Avenue up to and including Greenwich Village. Real estate had become a third empire for Astor, after fur trading and shipping, and it would be the most profitable by far, leaving him at his death in 1848 with an estate of 20 to 30 million dollars.

During General Mapes's lifetime in New York City, Astor, five years his senior, was the most significant businessman and one of the most successful in the whole country. He and his associate Stephen Girard from Philadelphia financed to a large degree the country's war of 1812. Astor had come to New York City from Germany in 1784, five years before Jonas Mapes arrived from Long Island. Astor lived much longer than Mapes, dying at age 85. He had the entrepreneur's instinct, investing primarily in city land rather than buildings or houses, with the important exception of the Astor House (built in 1836), the City Hotel and a few others.

Other notable developments occurred in 1828. In January the trustees of Columbia College established a grammar school to be preparatory to the college. The trustees felt that the various private seminaries in the city were not preparing students adequately for the course of study at Columbia. The Columbia Grammar School, became a leading private school in the city. Students were under the direction of a Columbia-appointed faculty and headmaster, and were charged a tuition of $12.50 per quarter!

Newgate, the state prison on the Hudson River in Greenwich Village, was closed, and prisoners were moved to a new prison up the river in Sing Sing (Ossining today). Astor's land in Greenwich Village was rapidly filling up with new houses, with the ground rent filling his purse.

On May 8, work began on the excavation of the Harlem Canal to run from Harlem Creek to Manhattanville. When completed this canal would in effect connect the Harlem River with the Hudson River, permitting the boat and barge traffic that exists today. Prior to that time only a small meandering stream connected the two rivers, and the Harlem River flowed south only to Hellgate.

Following completion of the Erie Canal in 1825, several other canals were dug to provide easier and cheaper transportation of goods. One of these of great importance to New York City was the Delaware and Hudson Canal, known as the "Anthracite Canal," which linked the Lackawanna Valley in Pennsylvania to Kingston on the Hudson River, enabling anthracite coal to be barged cheaply to the city. On December 10, 1828, the first barge of this fuel arrived from Kingston; soon immense quantities of both coal and wood followed to the city's wharves and yards.*

During that same year the first edition of *Webster's Dictionary* was published in New York. The author, Noah Webster, had started writing it in 1807 and was 70 years old at its completion. It was the first dictionary compiled in the United States, containing 70,000 headwords in two volumes of 1,600 pages in total.

A new political era came to the nation on November 4, 1828, with the election of the hero of the Battle of New Orleans, Andrew Jackson, a Democrat, as president. Jacksonian democracy would dominate politics for several decades. In New York State Martin Van Buren, with views similar to Jackson's, was elected governor, succeeding DeWitt Clinton, who died in office on February 10. Clinton's passing ended his control of state affairs for most of the last 25 years. Van Buren, however, only served one year as governor before moving to Washington to be Jackson's secretary of state (1829), vice president (1832), and then president (1836).

In New York City, William Paulding was chosen mayor by the Common

---

* In 1854 alone over one million tons of Pennsylvania coal came down the Delaware and Hudson Canal.

Council again in 1828, succeeding diarist Philip Hone. Paulding had been mayor in 1824, 1825, and 1826. It wasn't until 1834 that mayors were elected by voters. Tammany democrats were dominant in the city by then and only in a few instances could the opposing Whig party win a mayoral election, usually after corruption became too noticeable. The Federalists had disappeared after the War of 1812 was over and were replaced by the Whig party as the principal opposition to the Democrats.

Neither DeWitt Clinton nor Jonas Mapes lived to see the railroad come to Manhattan, an event that would transform transportation both within as well as to and from the booming metropolis. On November 14, 1832, the New York and Harlem Railroad began service using a horse-drawn car on a track connecting Union Square with 23rd Street and 4th Avenue. The city required that trains and trolleys be pulled by horses south of 32nd Street. This track, only nine blocks long, was the beginning of carriages carrying people on tracks, the forerunner of today's trains and subways.

SOURCE NOTES

1. Primary source papers of Mary Mapes Dodge, as found in her biography by Catherine Morris Wright (see endnote 22).

2. New England Historical and Genealogical Register 55/378.

3. John Lion Gardiner, *Gardiners of Gardiner's Island*, 1927, p. 3.

4. Belle Barstow, *Setauket, alias Brookhaven*, Author House, 2004, p. 19.

5. Ralph Hawkins, *A Hawkins Genealogy 1635–1939*, 1939.

6. J. Wickham Case, Southold Town Records, 1882.

7. Edwin P. Adkins, *Setauket: The First Three Hundred Years, 1655–1955*, Three Village Historical Society, Setauket, New York, 1980.

8. Belle Barstow, *Setauket, alias Brookhaven*, op. cit., 2004.

9. Long Island Records of Town of Brookhaven, Dec. 8, 1663.

10. William S. Pelletreau, *A History of Long Island*, Vol. II, 1903, p. 254.

11. Beverly C. Tyler, Chair, Three Villages Historical Society in *The Three Village Herald*, April 11, 2001, p. 9.

12. New York Genealogical and Biographical Society, *Record*, Vol. 134, p. 27.

13. Edwin P. Adkins, *Setauket — The First Three Hundred Years*, 1980 edition, p. 40.

14. Morton Pennypacker, *Washington's Spies on Long Island and New York*, 1939, pp. 11, 55.

15. Charles E. Craven, *History of Mattituck*, Amereon Ltd. (1988 reprint).

16. Pennypacker, op. cit.

17. Eric Homberger, *The Historical Atlas of New York City*, 1994, pp. 51, 56.

18. Molly Cadwell Crosby, *The American Plague*, 2006.

19. Alexander C. Flick, *History of New York*, Vol. V, 1934, pp. 225–28.

20. *The Memorial History of the City of New York*, Vol. V, pp. 321–25.

21. James Riker, *History of Harlem: Its Origin and Early Annals*, New Harlem Publishing Company, 1881, p. 715.

22. Catherine Morris Wright, *Lady of the Silver Skates*, Clingstone Press, Jamestown R.I., 1979, p. 2.

23. *Papers of Alexander Hamilton*, Vol. 26, p. 114.

24. Edwin G. Burrows and Mike Wallace, *Gotham*, Oxford University Press, 1999, p. 384.

25. Hawkins family archives

26. I.N. Phelps Stokes, *Iconography of Manhattan Island*, Vol. III, p. 505.

27. Rocellus S. Guernsey, *New York City and Vicinity during the War of 1812–1815*, Vol. II, 1889.

28. Guernsey, Vol. II, pp. 23–25.

29. Guernsey, Vol. II, pp. 177–80.

30. Guernsey, Vol. II, p. 537.

31. Guernsey, Vol. II, p. 339.

32. *Gotham*, p. 428.

33. Warren M. Hoffnagle, *Road to Fame: William H. Harrison and the Northwest*, The Ohio State Museum, 1959.

34. Guernsey, Vol. II, p. 312.

35. Pub. Papers of Daniel D. Tompkins III, p. 554.

36. Minutes of Common Council, October 10, 1814.

37. A. J. Langguth, *Union 1812*, Simon and Schuster, 2006, p. 340.

38. Guernsey, Vol. II, pp. 373–375.

39. Guernsey, Vol. II, pp. 383–85.

40. T. R. Roosevelt, *The Naval War of 1812*, New York, 1999.

41. Guernsey, Vol. II, pp. 437–8.

42. Stokes, Vol. V, p. 1580.

43. Pub. Papers of Daniel D. Tompkins I, pp. 519–20.

44. D. S. Alexander, *Political History of the State of New York*, Vol. I, 1906, p. 219.

45. Alexander C. Flick, *History of the State of New York*, Vol. V, p. 224.

46. Charles H. Wilson, *Wanderer in America*, Thirsk, 1822, pp. 14–16.

47. *New York Evening Post*, December 4–5, 1816.

48. Baron Axel Leonhard Klinckowstrom, "A description by a Swedish visitor in 1818."

49. Catherine Morris Wright, op. cit., pp. 2, 3.

50. John Palmer, *Journal of Travels in the United States of North America and in Lower Canada, Performed in the year 1817*, 1818, Sherwood, Neely, and Jones, London.

51. Proceedings of American Antiquarian Society, 94:241-67.

52. Doris Kearns Goodwin, *Team of Rivals*, 2005 p. 91.

53. *Gotham*, p. 430.

55. *New York Evening Post*, Sept. 4–5, 1822.

56. Ibid.

57. Common Council Minutes.

58. *New York Evening Post*, Oct. 26, 1822.

59. *New York Evening Post*, July 20, 1824.

60. *New York Evening Post*, Aug. 17–18, 1824.

61. James Fenimore Cooper, *Notions of the Americans: Picked up by a Travelling Bachelor*, London, 1928, pp. 240–46.

62. Catherine Morris Wright, op. cit., p. 2.

63. Cadwallader D. Colden Memoir, 1825.

64. *Gotham*, p. 430.

65. *New York Mirror*, III, pp. 126–7.

66. Laws of New York State.

67. *Gotham*, p. 547.

68. Will of Jonas Mapes.

69. Catherine Morris Wright, op. cit., p. 4.

70. Andrew T. Goodrich, *The Picture of New York and Strangers Guide to the Commercial Metropolis of the United States*, A.T. Goodrich, 1828.

The photographs of American Historical Prints are from the collection of the author and from the Phelps Stokes Collection —The New York Public Library.

INDEX

Women are listed under their birth names, with the married name in parentheses, e.g. "Tylee (Mapes), Elizabeth." Buildings and streets listed here are located in New York City, unless otherwise noted. Italic page numbers refer to illustrations.

Adams, John, 64
Adams, John Quincy, 97
African Americans
  in New York City, 48
  segregation of, 142–43
  slaves, 34, 36
African Free School, 143
Albany, New York, 69, 137, 141
Alexandria, Virginia, 92
Allen, Stephen, 125
American Revolution. *See* War of Independence
André, John, 37
anthracite coal, 141, 155
Anti-Loyalist Act of 1784, 54
Apprentices' Library, 123
Aquebogue, Long Island, 26, 31, 35
Armstrong, Secretary of War John, 11, 84, 91
Arnold, Aaron, 129, 142
Arnold, Benedict, 37
Arnold, Constable & Co., 129, 142
Astor, John Jacob, 52, 71, 74, 129, 154

Bank for Savings, 118–19
Bank of New York, 48
banks, 118–19
Batchelor (ship), 18
Battle of Lake Champlain, *95*
Battle of Lake Erie, 77
Battle of Long Island, 75
Battle of New Orleans, 100–103
Battle of Waterloo, 103
Bayard, William, 118, 119, 135, 137, 138
Bayard family, 129
Beekman family, 50
beer, 52–53

Bermuda, 76, 82, 83, 96, 98
biblical names, 20
Biggs, Thomas, 30
Biggs (Hawkins), Mary, 30, 33
Bill of Rights (U.S. Constitution), 53
Bonnington, Sir Matthew, 18
Boston, Massachusetts, 19–20
Bowery Village, 68
Bremner, Andrew, 90
Brewster, Caleb, 37
Brewster, Reverend Nathaniel, 29–30
Brewster, Elder William, 29
Bridewell Prison, 45, 60
Britain, U.S. relations with, 73
British fleet
  blockade of New York Harbor, 74, 76, 103
  ships of, 78–79
  threat to New York City (War of 1812), 12
British troops
  evacuation from New York City (War of Independence), 45
  garrisoning in Long Island towns, 37
  occupation of Eastern Long Island, 36–38
Broad Street, *47*, 112–16
Broadway, 50, 112, *113, 148*, 153–54
Brookhaven (Setauket), Long Island, 23, 28–29, 32
Brooklyn
  ferry to, 60
  forts in, 89
  threat to, from British invasion, 86
Brooks, Lord, 18
Brown and Bell, 141
Buffalo, New York, 76, 120, 137, 141
Burr, Aaron, 49, 53, 63–64
businesses, mass production methods in, 72–73

Calhoun, John, 73
Canada
  U.S. invasion of (1812), 76
  boundary with, 97
  British invasion from (1814), 94

CATHERINE D. HAVEMEYER

HARRY W. HAVEMEYER is a fourth-generation resident of
the Town of Islip, Long Island, where he has lived with his wife for
57 years. He has previously written a trilogy on the history of the
Great South Bay and several books on family history.